MODELS
IN PLANNING

An Introduction to the Use of
Quantitative Models in Planning

MODELS IN PLANNING

An Introduction to the Use of
Quantitative Models in Planning

C. LEE

DEPARTMENT OF TOWN AND COUNTRY PLANNING
UNIVERSITY OF NEWCASTLE

PERGAMON PRESS

OXFORD · NEW YORK · TORONTO
SYDNEY · BRAUNSCHWEIG

Pergamon Press Ltd., Headington Hill Hall, Oxford

Pergamon Press Inc., Maxwell House, Fairview Park, Elmsford,
New York 10523

Pergamon of Canada Ltd., 207 Queen's Quay West, Toronto 1

Pergamon Press (Aust.) Pty. Ltd., 19a Boundary Street,
Rushcutters Bay, N.S.W. 2011, Australia

Vieweg & Sohn GmbH, Burgplatz 1, Braunschweig

First edition 1973

Library of Congress Cataloging in Publication Data

Lee, Colin.
   Models in planning.

   (Urban and regional planning series, v. 4)
   1. Cities and towns—Planning—Mathematical
models. I. Title. II. Series.
HT166.L44 1973   309.2′62   72–8442
ISBN 0–08–017020–X
ISBN 0–08–017021–8 (flexicover)

Printed in Great Britain by Bell and Bain Ltd., Glasgow

**Urban and Regional Planning Series
Volume 4**

ISBN 0 08 017021 8 (flexicover)
ISBN 0 08 017020 X (hard cover)

Contents

Acknowledgements

THE need for an introductory text of this kind was suggested by George Chadwick, and I would like to express my appreciation for his suggestions and encouragement. The approach adopted here has evolved over a number of years of teaching graduate and undergraduate students, and owes much to the comments, questions and suggestions from students. The development of my ideas has also been influenced by colleagues in planning practice and education, and I would particularly like to acknowledge my gratitude to Bob Coursey for his helpful discussions, suggestions and criticism.

My particular thanks are due to Margaret Bell, who typed most of the draft; also to Greta Duke and Elaine Capstaff, who provided assistance in difficult circumstances.

Finally, I must thank my wife for her support and encouragement, and her patient endurance of many working nights and weekends.

Newcastle upon Tyne   COLIN LEE

Introduction

SINCE the mid-1960s there has been an increasing interest in, and use of, quantitative models of urban and regional systems. The development of operational models for use in urban planning means that both students and practising planners need to familiarise themselves with modelling techniques. There are many descriptions of the individual models which have been developed in planning and research studies in this country and elsewhere, but invariably these descriptions assume a level of numerate ability which the majority of planners do not possess. Experience suggests that planning students find considerable difficulty in coming to terms with quantitative models and there is a danger that the reaction to these difficulties will prevent a full appreciation of the significance and limitations of operational models. The objective of this book is to provide an introduction to some of the techniques which are being used to construct urban and regional models, for students and practising planners with a limited numerate background.

This is not a mathematical textbook for planners. The emphasis throughout is on the understanding of model structure rather than on rigorous mathematical analysis. Nevertheless, it is impossible to deal with quantitative models without some contact with the language and methods of mathematics.

In recognition of the difficulties which many people experience in dealing with numerate methods, the method of presentation attempts to help the reader assimilate the subject-matter step-by-step: all of the mathematical operations and symbols used in the models are explained before the models themselves are introduced, and each model to be examined is presented both verbally and mathematically, and a simple practical example is worked through in detail.

No attempt is made to provide a comprehensive analysis of urban and regional models: this is an introductory text, and attention is deliberately restricted to the basic forms of the most frequently used *spatial* models. All of the models to be discussed are models for predicting the location of activities within urban regions or the interactions between activities once the level of activities has been determined. The range of models which are available for forecasting the *levels* of urban activities are not dealt with.

It is hoped that after completing the text, readers will be able to follow up the extensive literature dealing with the more complex operational versions of the models discussed here.

CHAPTER 1

The Role of Models in the Planning Process

THERE is a growing acceptance that the use of models can help the planner to understand and, in appropriate circumstances, predict the behaviour of urban systems. However, models represent only a small (although increasingly important) part of planning methodology, and it is important for the potential model-builder and user to appreciate the place of this particular aspect of methodology within the wider context of the planning process as a whole. This chapter therefore begins with a brief examination of the planning process, both in conceptual terms and in terms of the statutory framework introduced by the 1968 Town and Country Planning Act. This is not an extensive or detailed analysis. It is introduced merely in order to identify the contribution which models can make to the work of the planner. The reader who wishes to obtain a more detailed understanding of the way in which these ideas have emerged should consult the works of Mitchell (1961), Chapin (1965), Chadwick (1966, 1971) and McLoughlin (1969).

THE PLANNING PROCESS

As Chadwick (1966) has pointed out: "planning is a conceptual general system. By creating a conceptual system independent of, but corresponding to, the real world system, we can seek to understand the phenomena of change, then to anticipate them and finally evaluate them—to concern ourselves with the optimisation of the real world system by seeking optimisation of the conceptual system."

1

There have been many attempts to identify a structure for the problem-solving process which is appropriate for guiding the planner in his search for optimal solutions. The writings of Patrick Geddes established the need for diagnosis before plan-making, although the plan was expected to emerge from the diagnostic process. With the establishment of the 1947 Town and Country Planning Act, the survey–analysis–plan rationale of planning was accepted and formalised, although the techniques of analysis which were employed were frequently rudimentary. Within the last fifteen to twenty years the methodology of systems analysis has been developed in scientific, industrial and military fields in an attempt to provide policy advice on the basis of systematic analytical studies. In more recent years there have been attempts to redefine the planning process in terms of the procedures of systems analysis, and there are signs of an emerging agreement about the components of what might be called the systemic planning process (the name "systemic planning" implies that the complex matters to be dealt with are system-like in their characteristics and behaviour, and that planning is to be carried out in a more systematic fashion).

Catanese and Steiss (1968) suggest that this process can be structured into seven major phases, as follows:

(i) Definition and clarification of current and future problems, and the inter-relationships among them.

(ii) Prediction of future conditions arising from identifiable problems.

(iii) Identification of parameters, boundary conditions or constraints which determine the range of possible solutions to the totality of problems.

(iv) Determination of goals and objectives at varying levels.

(v) Formulation of alternative policies.

(vi) Evaluation of qualitative and quantitative costs and effectiveness, and simulation of alternatives in the environment of the urban system, in order to understand overall performance, as well as by-products and spill-over effects.

(vii) Recommendation of selected policy and implementation.

This corresponds fairly well with the metaprocedure outlined by Chadwick (1969):

(i) Recognition and description of the system.

(ii) Formulation of criteria for testing the system.

(iii) Modelling the system.

(iv) Testing the system model against the criteria.

(v) Choosing a projected future state from the model.

(vi) Testing the projected future state against the criteria.

(vii) Controlling the system's behaviour towards the desired future state.

Although there are minor differences between these and other formulations of the systemic planning process, it seems that some agreement is emerging about the essential components of a framework for planning. An examination of alternative frameworks suggests that a consensus view might be represented by the following sequence:

(i) System description and problem definition.

(ii) Solution generation and analysis.

(iii) Evaluation and choice.

(iv) Implementation and monitoring.

(i) System description and problem definition

Description of the system involves an identification of the system of interest to the planner. This consists of a recognition of the variables considered to be relevant in order to understand the structure and performance of the existing system. This can be thought of as a process of system modelling—an attempt to reduce the variety (detail or complexity) of the system to a level which can be managed and comprehended. The problem definition consists of an assessment of system performance in relation to system objectives and standards, and system constraints.

(ii) Solution generation and analysis

The aim of the solution generation stage should be to generate a range of solutions which satisfy the previously determined objectives to a greater or lesser degree, without violating the constraints. There is no generalised approach to solution generation. Chadwick (1969) provides a useful review of the alternative approaches available for generating alternatives. Amongst the alternatives that he considers, the most frequently used are described in the following extract:

"The generation of alternatives can be done in several ways. We can start from the existing system and simply try to 'solve' its present problems, although in doing so we run the risk of ignoring change in the system which may lead to further, as yet unforeseen, problems. Such an approach would begin with models of the present system and simply try to modify them to eliminate known 'lack of fit' (i.e. the difference between existing performance of the system and system objectives). . . . In a planning situation several further starting points for the invention of alternatives seem to be useful. We might start, for example, with theories which appear to explain present relationships between activities, and then evolve future sets of relationships which preserve those attributes which seem likely to be constantly valuable. For example, in a regional system, we may seek an explanation of spheres of influence of certain service centres, and of rank-size relationships, in Location Theory, and use this theory as the basis for similar relationships in the future system. Theories of urban form may also be used, although such theories are often lacking in explanatory rigour. Another approach found to be useful is based upon the concept of broad relationships between major activities, described in terms such as 'dispersed', 'concentrated', with possible combinations. From such broad concepts, broad criteria of satisfaction can be judged, before more specifically regional site/location oriented models are conceived."

The solution analysis phase aims to predict the probable operating characteristics of each of the alternatives, i.e. to assess the magnitudes of the system variables and their interactions.

(iii) Evaluation and choice

The aim of this stage is to identify the solution or policy which best satisfies the system objectives. In fact the process of "inventing the future", as represented by the previous stage, may well cause some of the objectives to be revised or expanded. It is also inevitable that, although this discussion has been cast in terms of "objectives" and "performance", there will be many decision areas where subjective decision and value judgement play large parts. In these circumstances the results of quantitative analysis are being used as aids to decision-making, and are not in themselves providing decisions.

(iv) Implementation and monitoring

The process of implementation is obviously one of the most important components of the planning process. If the machinery for implementation is inadequate, even the most soundly based policy will be ineffective. The significance of monitoring, however, has only recently begun to be fully appreciated. It is important to be able to test the behaviour and the characteristics of the system at frequent intervals to check that the assumptions and objectives of the policy remain valid. Monitoring is the means by which the relevance of planning policy can be maintained.

There is a direct relationship between the conceptual views of the planning process which have emerged in recent years, and the changes in the statutory planning process introduced by the Town and Country Planning Act of 1968. This is not to say that the changing conceptual view was the cause of the statutory changes; simply that the result of the new legislation is to incorporate into the statutory planning framework many of the features which are associated with the "systems view" of the planning process.

The essential change proposed for the planning system was the distinction between policy (or strategic) decisions at coarse geographical scale on the one hand, and the more detailed local design and environmental decisions on the other. The development plans to be submitted to the Minister of Housing and Local Government are plans dealing with the broad structure of an area. These are called structure plans, and they are concerned with the policies for directing and controlling the growth and change of the urban system in accordance with a set of objectives.

The Department of the Environment (1970) has published a manual giving advice on the form and content of development plans. An examination of that section of the manual relating to the form and content of structure plans provides an interesting comparison with the statement of the systems planning framework outlined above.

The term "structure" is defined in the manual to mean "the social, economic and physical sub-systems of an area, so far as they are subject to planning control or influence. The structure is, in effect, the planning framework for an area, and includes such matters as the distribution of population, the activities and the relationships between them, the patterns of land use and the development the activities give rise to, together with the network of comunications and the systems of utility services." The manual then advises that a structure plan should be presented under the following collective headings:

(A) *Context of the plan*, with sections describing:
   (i) the national and regional setting, being an explanation of how national and regional policies have been interpreted by the plan;
   (ii) the sub-regional framework, being a description of the sub-regional context and decisions taken jointly with neighbouring authorities working in a sub-regional or conurbation grouping.

(B) *Existing structure*, an analysis of the existing structural components of the area, and the ways they inter-relate and relate to adjoining areas.

(C) *The aims of the plan*, a statement of goals and intentions.

(D) *The strategy of the plan*, including the reasoning behind, and description and comparison of alternatives, evaluated against objectives and resources.

The ideas that underlie the Ministry's advice on the preparation of structure plans, and the systems view of planning, are based on an understanding of system behaviour and on the preparation and evaluation of alternative strategies.

As McLoughlin (1969) points out, the preparation of alternative plans must be based on an understanding of how the urban system works, how it might evolve, how it would develop if left alone, and how it would react to different policies. However, urban systems are so complex that the description, analysis and prediction of their behaviour are formidable tasks. In order to reduce the complexity of urban systems to a manageable level, planners have recently begun to develop and use quantitative models. The purpose of the remainder of this introductory chapter is to briefly consider the nature of models, and their use within the planning process as described above.

THE NATURE OF MODELS

Essentially, a model is a representation of reality. It is usually a simplified and generalised statement of what seem to be the most important characteristics of a real-world situation; it is an abstraction from reality which is used to gain conceptual clarity—to reduce the variety and complexity of the real world to a level we can understand and clearly specify. The value of a model is that it can be used to improve our understanding of the ways in which a system behaves in circumstances where it is not possible (for technical, economic, political or moral reasons) to construct or experiment with a real-world situation.

Models can be classified in many ways, but a basic distinction is that between physical and abstract models. Physical models are perhaps more easily understood, and the ones with which most people will be familiar. They are usually scaled-down replicas of the objects under study. Aircraft designers, for example, used scaled-down models which can be tested and destroyed in the wind-tunnel at small cost, in order to form conclusions about the probable flight characteristics of the full-size aircraft. Similarly town planners and architects have for many years used scaled-down physical models in the solution of civic design problems.

An abstract model is one in which a real world situation is represented by symbols rather than by physical devices. Abstract models are much more useful to the planner than physical models when he turns his attention from the three-dimensional aspects of design to the representation of functional relationships and the basic processes of urban change.

Physical models are severely limited in their ability to describe the kind of system behaviour in which the planner is interested, whereas abstract models lend themselves well to behavioural analysis. Abstract, or symbolic, models are therefore the more important type of model for planning purposes.

Abstract models are in fact much more common than physical models, but, because they have many forms, they may not be recognised as such. The use of man's reasoning faculty invariably involves reference to abstract models. Rational behaviour involves examining the possible consequences of alternative courses of action, and selecting that which appears to provide the greatest benefits. This involves having in our minds a representation of the situation in which we are interested, and of what might happen next. This representation is an abstract model of the real situation. It can be a mental image or a verbal or written description, but whatever its form, it is the means by which we describe to ourselves or to others a real system or process. A manager deals continuously with mental and verbal models of the firm. Planners deal continuously with models of the urban system or its component parts. They may not be aware that they are using a model, and their models are not necessarily correct. They are simply constructs to substitute in our thinking for the real system that is being represented.

However, the purpose of this book is to examine a special type of abstract model, the mathematical model. Like other abstract models, a mathematical model is a description of the system it represents, but it is written in the "language" of mathematical symbols. Mathematical notation is a more precise language than English. Because it is less ambiguous, a mathematical model is a description which has greater clarity than most verbal models. Notice that "more precise" and "less ambiguous" do not mean "more accurate". When building a model, we start with a mental image, create a verbal description, and translate that verbal description into mathematical language. The accuracy of the description is dependent upon our ability to perceive the real-world system clearly. The mathematical formulation is simply a translation of our perceived view of the real world into another language. There is nothing inherent in the symbols of mathematics which guarantees accuracy. However, the precision required to translate words into symbols can often reveal inadequacies in the verbal description, and may thus lead to a sharpening-up or clarification of our mental image of the way in which we think the real-world system operates. This demand for precise and rigorous analysis is one of the most significant advantages of using mathematical models. We all use models, in the form of mental images. Translating these mental images into a precise mathematical formulation forces us to examine and set down clearly exactly how we think the system we are concerned with does work.

No mention has yet been made of the use of computers in developing and using models, although in reality almost all operational urban models rely on a computer for their effective use. This is simply because models of the urban system (or parts of it) are likely to be fairly complex, and require large amounts of repetitive calculation. The main characteristic of computers is that they are capable of performing calculations at high speed and with high degrees of accuracy. It therefore seems sensible to utilise this capacity as a tool in the construction of urban models.

Lowry (1965) makes the following comments on the way in which computers can be used in the model-building process:

"The model-builder can make use of this capacity for performing the most monotonous and repetitive tasks at high speed and with absolute mechanical accuracy only insofar as he is able to perceive repetitive temporal patterns in the processes of urban life, fixed spatial relationships in the kaleidoscope of urban form.

"If he can identify such stable relationships he may then find it possible to use them as building-blocks or elements of a computer model. These elements, replicated many times, can be combined and manipulated by the computer (according to rules specified by the model-builder) to generate larger, quasi-unique patterns of urban form and process which resemble those of the real world. The model literally consists of 'named' variables embedded in mathematical formulae (structural relations), numerical constants (parameters), and a computational method programmed for the computer (algorithm). The pattern generated is typically a set of values for variables of interest to the planner or decision-maker, each value tagged by geographical location and/or calendar date of occurrence."

Essentially, therefore, computers represent a means of making models operational, especially where the model is a large and complex one. They do not effectively alter the process of model building except that they require the mathematical formulation of the model to be re-expressed, first as an algorithm and then as a computer program. They may, however, because of the increased computational power which they provide, enable much more complex relationships to be evaluated than if the model-builder had to rely on mental arithmetic or hand-calculating machines.

MODELS IN THE PLANNING PROCESS

James Hester (1970) suggests that it is possible to identify two complementary, but sometimes conflicting, objectives for the use of models in urban planning. The first is a desire to uncover the dynamics of urban development, for its own sake, as a means of advancing the theory of urban growth, and making theory operational so that it can be refined and tested. This is equivalent to using models to describe or explain the behaviour of existing systems, and may therefore be very relevant to the "system description and problem definition" stage of the planning process as described on page 3. The second is a desire to use models as a means of projecting the future state of the systems they describe, in order to anticipate or influence the course of urban development in accordance with public policy. This may be related closely to the "generation and analysis of alternatives" phase of the planning process examined on page 3, and the preparation of alternative strategies as suggested in the Department of the Environment's Development Plans Manual (HMSO, 1970). The use of models within the planning process, therefore, would seem to be relevant to understanding the behaviour of urban systems (system description) and to the elaboration of alternatives (system forecasting). Hester (op. cit.) recognises that there is not *necessarily* a conflict between these two roles, for a model which is to be used for projection and the design of future systems must also be capable of describing and explaining the existing system. Similarly, a good descriptive model will often help in the development of a forecasting model. However, Forrester (1961) suggests that it is quite common to find that models which have been developed with only explanation in mind have often had their goals set so low that they are not only of no use for projection, but they also fail to provide an adequate description of system behaviour.

The recognition that models may have to satisfy different requirements according to the task for which they will be used has led Lowry (*op. cit.*) to suggest that mathematical models may be further classified into three categories. In Lowry's words, models "may fall into any of three classes, depending on the interests of the client and the ambition of the model-builder. In ascending order of difficulty these are: descriptive models, predictive (or forecasting) models, and planning models." This distinction is sufficiently important to warrant further explanation, and we will now examine each of Lowry's suggested categories in turn.

Descriptive models, as their name implies, are concerned solely with representing an existing situation. As Lowry (*op. cit.*) says:

"The builder of a descriptive model has the limited objective of persuading the computer to replicate the relevant features of an existing urban environment or of an already-observed process of urban change. . . . Good descriptive models are of scientific value because they reveal much about the structure of the urban environment, reducing the apparent complexity of the observed world to the coherent and rigorous language of mathematical relationships. They provide concrete evidence of the ways in which 'everything in the city affects everything else', and few planners would fail to benefit from exposure to the inner workings of such models. They may also offer a short-cut to fieldwork by generating reliable values for hard-to-measure variables from input data consisting of easy-to-measure variables."

An example of the latter use, described by Bayliss (1968), is the use of a descriptive model to provide information on household income, which is an invaluable variable in many areas of planning, but is notoriously difficult to collect. It has been found, however, that there is a close relationship between household income and other easily measured variables. It is possible to formalise and quantify this relationship, and when this has been done (on the basis of a sample survey, perhaps) the model can be used to provide information on household income over wider areas. It may be found that the relationship between household income and other variables is of the form:

$$I_n = a + b \cdot S_n + c \cdot R_n + d \cdot Z_n$$

where I_n = average household income in zone n,

   S_n = a function of the socio-economic structure of the heads of household in zone n,

   R_n = average rateable value of residential properties in zone n,

   Z_n = average household size in zone n,

   a, b, c and d are constants to be determined empirically.

It may be argued that a model such as this could be used for short-term forecasting, and as such can be regarded as a forecasting model. However, if we examine its limitations, some of the differences between descriptive and forecasting models will become apparent:

   (i) The variable R_n (average rateable value) is a function of institutional policies on how to calculate rateable values, and also of variations in the housing market. If either of these two factors change (as they do from time to time) then the relationship between rateable value and income is obviously altered.

(ii) Further unreliability would be introduced by changes in average family size and changes in accepted social customs (e.g. working wives, extension of further education) which would obviously distort the relationship between household size and household income.

Therefore although some models may be capable of adequately describing or reproducing existing urban systems or their component parts, they are not necessarily capable of use as predictive models. As Lowry (*op. cit.*) concludes: "Descriptive models do not directly satisfy the planner's demand for information about the future, or help him to choose among alternative programs. For these purposes he must look to the more ambitious predictive and planning models."

Predictive models, because they are required to simulate future rather than current situations, have much more stringent requirements than descriptive models, although they may operate in much the same way.

(i) Whereas descriptive simulation models can use almost any relationship in any way to describe a situation, only relationships which can be expected to remain reasonably constant over time should be used in forecasting models.

(ii) A forecasting model should be constructed so that the cause and effect phenomena take up their proper roles. For example, it might be found that there is a reciprocal relationship between car ownership and infant mortality, but it would be foolish to use this relationship for forecasting even though it adequately describes existing levels of car ownership. A much more reliable variable would be disposable household income, and, in forecasting, income must play the role of cause, and car ownership that of effect (in statistical terminology, car ownership is the dependent variable and income the independent variable). This is clearly obvious, but there will be many situations where it is not so easy to discern what is cause and what is effect, or even where cause and effect cannot be clearly separated because a state of interaction exists between all the variables. In this kind of situation the art of model-building can become very complex, and the results must be interpreted with a great deal of caution.

(iii) It is also necessary to ensure that the variables included in the model can be reasonably evaluated as far into the future as necessary. There is no point at all in having a sophisticated model which requires as inputs the future values of variables which are little better than guesses. The model developed for the San Francisco Community Renewal Program, for example, requires for each biennium of an 18-year forecasting period a prediction of the numbers of households in each of 114 socio-economic categories.

(iv) There is an important exception to this requirement, as pointed out by Lowry (*op. cit.*):

"This . . . requirement is partly relaxed in the case of conditional prediction . . . (when) the planner is interested in the state of the world following some contemplated act on his part. The model may then be allowed to respond in the form 'if X occurs, then Y will follow', without explicitly asserting the likelihood of X's occurrence.

"A special case of conditional prediction is called 'impact analysis'. Here, the interest is focussed on the consequence that should be expected to follow a specified exogenous impact (change in X) if the environment were otherwise undisturbed."

Planning models, or normative models, can perhaps be considered as extensions to forecasting models, but they have one very significant difference—they are constructed in such a way as to tell us not simply what is likely to happen as a result of certain assumptions, but rather what range of performance is possible in relation to defined objectives. This means, of course, that a planning model must have built into it certain goals and constraints. The model might for example be designed to produce the plan which has the least capital cost, or which keeps journeys to work at a minimum, or to provide maximum accessibility to the central area. It might have constraints built into it about the density of development to be allowed, about the location of certain kinds of uses, about the amounts of traffic to be generated within a given area, or about the maximum journey to work that can be permitted. The output of this kind of model is very much a reflection of what the planner thinks is desirable rather than a simple projection of "natural forces", and as such it is likely to prove, ultimately, the most valuable kind of model. However, there are at this point in time very severe technical limitations on the use of normative models in planning. These limitations are associated less with the purely mathematical techniques of solution (which are complex, but manageable with high-capacity computers) than with the determination of objective measures for standards, costs and a wide range of attitudes and behavioural patterns which must be included in the model.

The use of predictive mathematical models as an aid to design, or the selection of policies in planning, is sufficiently important to examine in a little more detail. We have seen that a mathematical model represents the behaviour of a real-world system by symbols and numbers. If we then alter the numbers in accordance with different policies, we can see the effects of these policies on the state of the system, as represented by the model.

The prospectus for the San Francisco Community Renewal Program describes the use of mathematical models in policy-making as follows:

"A model is developed by examining the relationships among various factors considered to be important in the workings of some total system. Some models are best expressed graphically, some verbally. When the relationships can best be expressed through numbers, the system is represented by a mathematical model. Expressing the quantified relationships between a set of inter-related factors, a mathematical model affords a simplified and manageable picture of the workings of the total system. A model is designed in such a way that if a change is made in one or several of its component factors, the resulting effect on the total picture can be measured.

"The basic idea behind the use of models is quite simple. Suppose we wanted to build a complex system of lines and pulleys to lift and move large weights from various points. If the system were really complex, we would be unable to trace out in our minds the consequences on the total system that would result from pulling any single line. In this case we might want to build a scale model with strings before we constructed the actual system. Using the scale model we could develop a pattern of string-pulling which could best accomplish our overall objectives, by testing each action in advance.

"A mathematical model operates in essentially the same fashion, except that the strings are replaced by numbers in the form of mathematical equations. Each equation represents a relationship that exists between the elements that constitute the city. By altering the numbers, and thus affecting the relationships, we can quickly see the effects of a proposed change." (Little, 1963.)

The potential of models in planning, in terms of their ability to help the planner to understand and predict the behaviour of urban systems, would seem therefore to be great, and the pace of model development in this country has increased rapidly since 1965. Enthusiasm for the use of models is widespread in professional and academic circles, and substantial funds are currently being directed to research into the application of models in planning.

It is perhaps advisable to correct an impression that is sometimes created, that the adoption of computer-aided models within the planning process implies the development of a "black-box" approach to planning—the situation in which the analyst feeds information into the box and obtains from it a series of alternatives and details of the costs and effectiveness of each alternative. This is quite rightly seen as a dangerous situation; a system which removes from the planner the ability to understand and control the process of urban growth and change would be most undesirable. But this view is based on a misunderstanding of the role of models and their application within a systems framework. The application of models to planning is not intended to replace expert judgement. It represents an attempt to provide "a systematic approach to helping a decision-maker choose a course of action by investigating his problem, searching out objectives and alternatives, and comparing them in the light of their consequences, using an appropriate framework—in so far as possible analytic—to bring expert judgement and intuition to bear on the problem" (Quade and Boucher, 1968).

There are, however, some inherent limitations on the use of models within the planning process. Even within the fields of scientific and industrial applications (which are perhaps more susceptible to rigorous quantitative analysis) it is recognised that "where model-building is an extremely systematic expedient to promote the understanding and control of our environment, reliance on the use of expert judgement, though often unsystematic, is more than an expedient: it is an absolute necessity. Expert opinion must be called on whenever it becomes necessary to choose among several alternative courses of action, in the absence of an accepted body of theoretical knowledge that would clearly single out one course as the preferred alternative. This can happen if there is either a factual uncertainty as to which of the consequent states of the world would be preferable. The latter kind of doubt often arises even when there is a clear-cut, basic ethical code, because the multiple moral implications of a complex change in the environment may not be directly assessable in terms of the basic code" (Helmer, 1966). How much more is this true of planning where the problems involve the relationship of a large number of variables associated with a plurality of goals that are simultaneously operative, and where some of the goals even defy clear definition, and many of the most important variables are intangible or non-quantifiable. There will always therefore be areas where the use of quantitative models is not an appropriate method of analysis.

It could perhaps be argued that a second limitation to the usefulness of models in planning is the absence of a well-defined body of theory in many of the areas in which we are interested. Britton Harris (1967) has defined a model as "an experimental design based on a theory" and if we accept this definition it is easy to see how limited the application of models must be. However, this is not a limitation of models *per se*; it is a limitation arising from the inability of the planner to understand and describe urban structure and the process of urban change. It is nevertheless a very real limitation on the use of models for operational purposes and one which is reflected in the title of a paper delivered in 1968, "Computation is not enough!" In this paper Britton Harris observed: "We cannot successfully exploit the very considerable capabilities of computers until we greatly increase our understanding of the world with which we are dealing and the means with which we will represent it and manipulate it inside the computer." It is important to note, however, that this limitation is one which applies to the use of models for operational purposes, at the present time. It is not an argument for refusing to undertake research into the application of models in an urban planning context. Indeed, unless urban models are used by researchers, it is unlikely that the body of theoretical knowledge about the way urban systems work will be substantially increased, for, in urban planning, as in other fields, models actually assist in the development of theory. What is needed in planning is more hypotheses about the way the urban system and its component parts operate. The use of models in research can help to overcome this shortage.

One of the major practical problems involved in the use of models is the limitations imposed by the availability of data. Even the simplest model can have a vast appetite for data, and the more realistic a model becomes, the more the appetite increases. Many planning studies in the United

States have foundered because of the problems of data availability and collection. This again is not an argument for abandoning models. It is, however, a warning that frequently the information required by models is not readily available from published sources, and elaborate, time-consuming and costly data-collection exercises are required.

The objective of this chapter has been to provide the context and background against which the more detailed problems of constructing and using models can be appreciated. Chapter 2 will consider some of the general principles which may be useful to the beginner of the model-building field.

REFERENCES

BAYLISS, D. (1968) *Some Recent Trends in Forecasting.* Centre for Environmental Studies Working Paper 17.

CATANESE, A. and STEISS, D. (1968) Systemic planning for very complex systems. *Planning Outlook*, new series, vol. 5.

CHADWICK, G. F. (1966) A systems view of planning. *Journal of the Town Planning Institute*, May.

CHADWICK, G. F. (1969) *A Method for Regional Planning.* (Mimeo.) University of Manchester, Dept. of Town and Country Planning.

CHADWICK, G. F. (1971) *A Systems View of Planning.* Pergamon Press.

CHAPIN, F. S. (1965) *Urban Land Use Planning.* Univ. of Illinois Press.

DEPT. OF THE ENVIRONMENT (1970) *Development Plans: A Manual of Form and Content.* H.M.S.O.

FORRESTER, J. W. (1961) *Industrial Dynamics.* M.I.T. Press

HARRIS, B. (1967) *Quantitative Models of Urban Development.* University of Pennsylvania.

HARRIS, B. (1968) *Computation is not enough!* Annual Address to Association for Computing Machinery.

HELMER, O. (1966) *Social Technology.* Basic Books Inc., New York.

HESTER, J. (1970) *Systems Models of Urban Growth and Development.* Urban Systems Laboratory, M.I.T.

LITTLE, ARTHUR D. (1963) *San Francisco Community Renewal Program—Purpose, Scope and Methodology.* Arthur D. Little Inc.

LOWRY, I. S. (1965) A short course in model design. *Journal of the American Institute of Planners.*

MCLOUGHLIN, J. B. (1969) *Urban and Regional Planning.* Faber & Faber.

MITCHELL, R. B. (1961) The new frontier in metropolitan planning. *Journal of the American Institute of Planners.*

QUADE, E. S. and BOUCHER, W. I. (Eds.) (1968) *Systems Analysis and Policy Planning.* Elsevier.

CHAPTER 2

Principles for the Design and Use of Models

IT is probably true to say that no one completely understands how a model is born. Nevertheless, it is possible to outline a general approach which may be helpful in the planning of a model-building exercise.

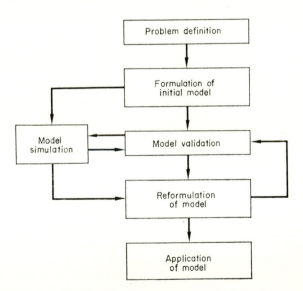

FIG. 2.1. Model development as an iterative process (after Hamilton *et al.*, 1969).

The application of a model to a real-word problem is not a simple process. Any step of the research involved in model development may suggest that earlier ideas may be improved on. It seems inevitable, therefore, that a realistic approach to model-building should be an iterative one, as suggested by Hamilton *et al.* (1969), and as shown in Fig. 2.1.

The iterative cycles during which the structure of the model is progressively refined can be thought of as being equivalent to the laboratory or wind-tunnel tests which engineers and scientists use to improve the design of physical models, with the physical tests being replaced by computer simulation runs of the model and interpretation and testing of the results. Simulation of the initial model may provide results which inadequately represent the real system which is being replicated, but which suggest lines for further research. Additional research may then yield a formulation which produces better results.

It is convenient to break the framework illustrated in Fig. 2.1 into five major steps (problem definition; model formulation; model simulation; model validation; and application of the model) although it must be emphasised that these steps are not self-contained or sequential activities. We will discuss each of them in turn for ease of exposition only.

PROBLEM DEFINITION

In common with other forms of research, the development of models for the simulation of urban systems should begin with the formulation of a problem or an explicit statement of the objectives of the exercise, for there is little benefit to be gained from building a model just for the sake of it. Care must be taken not to build a model of an urban system without an end in mind, for a model is a means to an end, and is not an end in itself. This may seem to be an obvious first step, but determining the problems and the objectives is the most critical part of almost any activity. The questions to be answered effectively control model design. The questions must be specific and clearly stated if the study is to progress satisfactorily, or many of the important decisions which have to be taken during the course of model formulation will be impossible to take (for example, unless there is a specific objective for the use of the model, it will be impossible to decide what variables must be included, or can reasonably be left out, or what level of aggregation is acceptable).

The critical questions which the model is to be used to answer must therefore be specified with a reasonable amount of detail at the beginning of the model-building process, even though they may be refined as the exercise progresses. As Forrester (1961) suggests: "Questions which are too general may fail to provide an adequate framework for research. Questions which are too narrow may restrict the investigation to areas which do not contain the answer." This is not to say that objectives cannot be broad, provided that their scope is appreciated. It would, for example, be perfectly reasonable to have as an objective the building of a model to understand the behaviour of a system, but it is important to recognise that the emphasis is on the understanding of phenomena, and not on the model itself.

The most common questions to which models have been applied in the urban planning field have been related to the levels and location of various activities, e.g. What is the future population of an urban area likely to be? What factors determine the location of population? How much shopping floorspace should be provided in a town centre? What are the likely volume and directions of journeys to work? Which highway network would best accommodate the journeys-to-work flows?

MODEL FORMULATION

The formulation of a model can be considered in five stages: selection of the variables to be included; choice of the appropriate level of aggregation and categorisation; decisions about the treatment of time; specification; calibration.

What variables to include?

One of the major difficulties in building a model is deciding what should be included, and what can safely be left out. A model should clearly be able to reproduce the phenomena in which its designer is interested, and an obvious answer therefore is to include those variables which are relevant to the problem, and to exclude everything else.

This is a starting point, but it still leaves the basic problem of deciding what the important variables and relationships are.

Many of the variables to be included will have been determined by the definition of the problem. These are the output variables, which must be included in the model. There will, however, be additional variables which, although not required as output from the model, are important because of the effect that they have on the output variables. If there is a strong causal relationship between a variable and one or more of the output variables, then it should be included in the model formulation. The model-builder must therefore have the imagination and the capacity to select the factors that he believes to be important, on the basis of his knowledge of a situation.

Level of aggregation and method of categorisation

Once it has been decided to include a variable, decisions have to be made about how to categorise the variable, and what level of aggregation is appropriate. Population, for example, may be classified by age, sex, occupation, place of residence, income, etc. The choice of a particular method of categorisation will be determined by the purpose of the model. A model for predicting car-ownership, for example, may need details of the population classified according to family size and income levels; on the other hand a model designed to forecast the level of the population in an area would be more concerned with the age and sex characteristics of population.

The level of aggregation which is acceptable in developing a model depends basically on two things: (a) whether the questions the model is designed to answer can in fact be answered in terms of aggregated variables, (b) whether the real-world relationships can be adequately represented by aggregates. It is easy to see how the level of aggregation may depend on the first of these questions. If the planner is interested in the age structure of the population as well as in its total size, the design of a population-forecasting model will have to be based on population disaggregated into the age groups in which the planner is interested.

However, the second of the above considerations—whether the real-world relationships can be adequately represented by aggregated variables—may mean that it is desirable to disaggregate population into age groups even if we are only interested in total population. This would be the case, for example, if the factors which determine the level of population—births, deaths and migration—have different effects on different age groups (as indeed they do). For example, in an area with a high unemployment rate, one would expect a much higher rate of migration among young adults, which affects not only the total population, but also the future structure of the population, because it is this group which produces the most children. A model which failed to disaggregate population into age groups would ignore any relationship of this kind which varies between age groups, and one would therefore have less confidence in its results.

The treatment of time

The way in which time is incorporated into the model is one of the most critical points of model design. It is also, unfortunately, one of the most difficult. There are two aspects of the treatment of time which are significant. The first is essentially a planning consideration, and is related to the time period for which the model is to be used—over what period are forecasts to be made, or in other words, what are the time horizons of the plan? The second aspect is concerned with the way in which the passage of time is accounted for in the model, and this is a much more difficult problem. It is partly a matter for planning consideration (for what points in time are outputs from the model needed?) and partly a question of model design (are changes in the relationships of the system components over time to be explicitly accounted for, or is the model to be essentially a static one?). It is known that urban change is a continuous process, and that the way in which urban areas change depends on the sequence in which development decisions are made. Models which describe a situation of continuous change are therefore likely to provide better representations of urban systems than models which describe an urban system at one point in time only. It is also desirable to have results from the model for intermediate points in time so that the way in which the urban system is likely to develop can be documented.

However, the development and operation of continuous change (dynamic) models is much more difficult than the construction of static (equilibrium) models and, although attention is now being turned towards the dynamic properties of urban systems, almost all of the models which have been used in planning situations to date have been of the static kind.

Specification of the model

By this stage, decisions will have been taken about the purposes for which the model is to be used. The need to specify the variables to be included, and to decide on the appropriate level of aggregation and method of categorisation, will have forced the model-builder to make some hypotheses, however tentative, about the structure and behaviour of the phenomena which he is trying to reproduce. The next step in model construction involves explicit description of the hypothesis (or hypotheses) of system behaviour, and the translation of this hypothesis into the appropriate mathematical or symbolic form. The obvious way to start is with a verbal description of the system with which one is dealing. This verbal model will describe the important features of the system and how they interact with each other. It provides the rationale for the hypothesis about system structure and behaviour which is being tested. When complete, the verbal description can then be translated into the equivalent formal mathematical model. This will rarely be a simple or straightforward process: unless an established hypothesis or operational model is being used, it will involve a choice of the most appropriate mathematical techniques, and this should not be attempted without the appropriate technical advice.

Calibration of the model

The specification of the model in mathematical terms will usually include various constants or parameters which add dimensions to the model's relationships (i.e. they specify *by how much* one variable changes in relation to the others).

If the form and structure of the model are satisfactory (e.g. if it has been used and proved on previous occasions), calibration is the relatively straightforward process of finding the value(s) of the parameter(s) which provide the best fit between the model and the observed situation. Where a new model is being developed the process of calibration cannot be conceived of in this simple way; it must rather be thought of in terms of the next two major stages of the model development process—simulation and validation. In this case the adjustments may well be to the basic relationships and the structure of the model, rather than only to parameter values, and the simple concept of calibration is not appropriate.

B

SIMULATION AND VALIDATION OF THE MODEL

Once the initial formulation of the model has been completed, its ability to reproduce the characteristics and behaviour of the real-world system must be tested. It is important to realise that the details of a model formulation may be altered as the understanding of the system being dealt with increases, and that computer simulation experiments with the initial model may contribute to this understanding. As a result of these experiments it may be necessary to amend or extend the initial formulation; this may be the case, for example, where the results of some particular relationship in the model produce results which seem unreasonable on the basis of past data and experience. If this does happen, then further investigation into the form of that relationship may be necessary (and that may involve the collection of additional data), and this in turn must be tested against the available data.

This iterative procedure, which is the core of the model-building process, involves frequent checks on the validity of the model. The subject of model validation is an extremely difficult one. There is little in the field of urban planning about which we have perfect information, so that we can never prove that a model is an exact representation of reality.

Because of the limitations of available data, therefore, model validation is extremely difficult. More important, however, as Forrester (1961) suggests, it is a relative judgement, for if it is impossible to say whether a model is an exact representation of reality, the adequacy of the model must be judged against the mental image or other representation which would be used instead. The question therefore is not a simple one of whether the model is valid or not. A model can be thought of as being successful if it helps to improve the accuracy with which we can represent reality. Testing for goodness of fit is therefore a critical step in model development. It is concerned with measuring the ability of the model to replicate the performance of its real-world counterpart within acceptable limits. This is obviously important, for any forecast or simulation is useless unless we have a measure of confidence of it. Validation, or the goodness of fit of the model, is some assurance that the model is doing what it was designed to do. There are four basic criteria against which any model can be evaluated:

(i) *Accuracy*. Obviously a model will be considered more likely to give correct forecasts of the future level or distribution of urban activities if it can re-create the existing situation correctly. The accuracy of model performance may be judged with the help of statistical measures, depending on the structure of the model being used, in order to compare certain critical aspects of the model's behaviour with the behaviour of the real-world system.

(ii) *Validity*. Although accuracy in terms of system behaviour is of obvious importance, the validity of the model's structure, in terms of the relationships between the variables, is of equal if not greater significance. The importance of model structure springs from the fact that if all of the system components are adequately described in the model, and if the inter-relationships are adequately specified, then the performance of the model can hardly fail to be accurate. On the other hand, it is not impossible for a variety of invalid combinations of components and relationships to produce apparently accurate behaviour, as compared to the existing system behaviour. It is unlikely, however, that an invalid structure will provide a sound guide to the future behaviour of urban systems. Each equation in the model should therefore express a reasonable relationship, preferably a direct causal relationship, between the variables incorporated in the model. The problem is how to identify the chain of cause and effect in a complex situation. However, the behaviour of the model is most likely to be valid if it is formulated on the basis of a reasoned hypothesis which has been subjected to rigorous testing.

(iii) *Constancy*. This criterion does not affect the value of the model as a descriptive device, but is of critical importance when the model is to be used for prediction. It is concerned with the extent to which the relationships which exist at present can be expected to remain constant over time. For some equations there may be no evidence either to suggest a change or to refute the possibility. For others, there may be indications that factors at present not included in the model will, in the future, have a much greater influence. Alternatively there may be a change in emphasis among the variables already included.

(iv) *Availability of estimates of variables*. Whether or not any model can be used successfully for forecasting depends on the availability of estimates of future values of the key variables. One of the considerations which should be borne in mind during the specification of the variables to be included in the model (and one which will certainly affect the accuracy of the model when used as a forecasting tool) is the ease and accuracy with which they can be forecast. Obviously there is little use in having a model which describes the existing situation very well, but when used for forecasting depends on the future values of variables which are little better than guesses (e.g. as mentioned on p. 13, a model of the San Francisco housing market developed by Arthur D. Little Inc. requires biennial estimates of the future population in 114 socio-economic categories).

APPLICATION OF THE MODEL

The method of application of a model, once it has been developed and satisfactorily tested, will depend on the circumstances in which it is used. It is, however, possible to suggest some of the ways in which models and their results can be integrated into the planning process. Bayliss (1968) suggests that "at the moment it is probably fair to say that with the crudity of current models, straightforward application is folly". It is not reasonable to expect any of the current generation of urban models to be able to make accurate forecasts of the specific state of future urban systems. They can, however, usefully be used to investigate the forces affecting urban development and to assess the likely directions of change. This understanding can be used to identify the probable behaviour of the system if present trends continue, or in the absence of positive policies to change the system's behaviour.

Bayliss (1968) goes on to outline the following steps as being most likely to produce the best results from the application of a model to a planning situation:

(i) Use the model (or models) to project the "natural" course of change in the urban system.

(ii) From this, isolate the "acceptable" and "objectionable" features.

(iii) Identify alternative patterns of development which are "desirable".

(iv) On the basis of these alternatives, policies may be formulated which should influence development in the desired direction.

(v) The effects of these policies can then be incorporated into the model, which can be run again to produce new forecasts. These forecasts must then be compared with the expected results, and if necessary the policies may have to be readjusted and modified in order to produce the desired results.

(vi) When a combination of policies has been devised which achieves the desired objectives, the alternative solutions generated by the model must be tested for feasibility and effectiveness, and the preferred alternative may be selected from this testing process.

Alternatively, models may be used in a slightly different way, either as a means of sensitivity analysis on a range of policies (as a means of testing by how much the policies may be varied without deviating significantly from the desired objectives), or as a means of testing the likely impact of major developments, such as a new employment or shopping centre, or the construction of an urban motorway.

The understanding of urban phenomena as an aid to the developing and testing of planning policy is the major objective of using models within the planning process. It is therefore important that their application should be carried out in a careful and sensitive manner. Later chapters will examine some of the better known or more frequently used models, and will work through some simple examples of their use, in order to provide an understanding and appreciation of the ways in which they operate, and the care with which they must be applied and their results interpreted. However, before considering specific models in detail, the next chapter will deal with some preliminary matters of terminology and symbols which may help the beginner to understand the subsequent examples.

REFERENCES

BAYLISS, D. (1968) *Some Recent Trends in Forecasting.* Centre for Environmental Studies Working Paper 17.

FORRESTER, J. W. (1961) *Industrial Dynamics.* M.I.T. Press.

HAMILTON, H. R. *et al.* (1969) *Systems Simulation for Regional Analysis.* M.I.T. Press.

CHAPTER 3

Mathematical Preliminaries

INTRODUCTION

The consideration of symbolic or mathematical models unavoidably involves some contact with the language or symbols of mathematics. This need not be a traumatic experience. The level of mathematical treatment in the models dealt with here is as simple as possible, and the purpose of this chapter is to present and explain only those elementary concepts and symbols which are necessary to understand the subsequent discussion of models. The discussion deals with the following topics:

   (i) Variables, constants and parameters.

  (ii) Relationships and functions.

 (iii) Subscripts.

 (iv) Summation signs.

  (v) Exponents.

 (vi) Solving equations.

VARIABLES, CONSTANTS AND PARAMETERS

Much of mathematics is concerned with operations on numbers (i.e. calculations of various kinds). Often, for convenience, we replace the numbers which refer to specific problems by general symbols which can represent a range of numbers. A *variable* is a symbol which can take on more than one value. For example, if we use the symbols N, B and D, to represent population change by natural increase, births and deaths respectively, we can say that:

$$N = B - D.$$

This is a general expression, and the variables N, B and D can take on any value, according to the context of the problem.

A *constant*, on the other hand, is a symbol or number which has only one value. In the formula to find the circumference of a circle, $C = 2\pi r$, the symbols 2 and π are constants: they remain the same whatever the problem, whereas the symbol r is a variable, the value of which varies according to the problem. A constant which will appear in some of the models to be discussed later is the exponential function e, which has a value of 2·71828 . . . whatever the particular problem in which it is used.

A *parameter*, on the other hand, is a symbol or a number the value of which may vary between problems, but is constant within a problem. For example, if we wanted to estimate population from the number of new houses built, and we knew what the dwelling occupancy rate in a given area was (the average number of people per dwelling), we would multiply the number of houses built, by the dwelling occupancy rate. In terms of symbols we might say:

$$P = H \times DOR.$$

In this case P and H are variables, and DOR is a parameter. It is a parameter rather than a constant because dwelling occupancy rates may vary between areas. Thus if there were two areas which had different dwelling occupancy rates $DOR1$ and $DOR2$, we could say that for the first area,

$$P = H \times DOR1$$

and for the second area

$$P = H \times DOR2.$$

For all houses in the first area, $DOR1$ is taken as a constant, but there is a different value of DOR for area two.

In all of these examples we are using letters of the alphabet as symbols to represent quantities. The expression

$$P = H \times DOR$$

has no meaning in itself. The meaning derives from the fact that we are using the letters to represent quantities. This is convenient because the relationship between population, number of houses and dwelling occupancy rate is true for any number of houses; it is a general relationship which can be represented in abstract terms by using letters to represent numbers. The models to be discussed in the following chapters are all based on general relationships, and can therefore be conveniently expressed using symbols.

MATHEMATICAL FUNCTIONS AND RELATIONSHIPS

Reference has already been made to the relationship between two variables. It was suggested above that there may be a relationship between population and dwellings—in other words population is somehow related to or depends on the number of houses. The way in which the two variables are related is described precisely in the expression

$$P = H \times DOR.$$

When a precise relationship such as this exists, which enables the value of one variable (P) to be found from the value of another variable, the relationship can be described as a functional relationship. More simply, P can be said to be some function of H. All that this means is that the value of P can be found by carrying out some operation on the value of H. In this particular case the operation which is carried out is to multiply H by a parameter, DOR. As we will see later it is possible to have very complex functions or relationships, but the meaning of the function is the same—the value of the variable on the left-hand side of the = sign is found by evaluating the expression on the right-hand side. The more complex the expression on the right-hand side, the more complex is the relationship between the variables.

When we describe a functional relationship by an equation, the variable on the left-hand side is called the dependent variable (its value *depends on* the values of the variables on the right-hand side), and the variables on the right-hand side are called independent variables.

The simple relationships that we have used up to now have been expressed as equalities: P is equal to $H \times DOR$. Some of the models that are described later use relationships which are not of this form, but will be based on inequalities. There are standard symbols for representing relationships which are based on inequalities, and the ones which will be used in later chapters are shown below:

$<$ means "is less than";

$>$ means "is greater than";

$\leqq$ means "is less than or equal to";

$\geqq$ means "is greater than or equal to".

For example, the expression

$$A \leqq B - 2$$

means that the two variables A and B are related in such a way that A is always less than or equal to $(B - 2)$.

SUBSCRIPTS

Many of the models we will be looking at will be concerned with a range of values for variables which apply to different areas. We might, for example, want to predict the population of not one area, but five different areas. In these cases we have to use a notation which helps us to identify any particular value from the general list. This notation is subscript notation. It is simply a means of identifying one element from a list of values. If we have five items or elements in a list, each one is given an identification number which describes its position in the list. If, for example, there were five areas for which we had population data, there would be five values of P. These would be identified using subscript notation as:

$$P_1, P_2, P_3, P_4, P_5$$

where the lowered numbers are subscripts.

If each of these five areas had different numbers of houses and different dwelling occupancy rates, then we would effectively need a separate equation describing the relationship for each area. For the first area, for example, we would say

$$P_1 = H_1 \times DOR_1$$

where the subscript reminds us that the value of the variables and parameters that we use must be those relating to the first area only.

If we want to discuss these numbers in general we may refer to an
element as P_i or P_j where the subscripts i and j are general subscripts,
i.e. they refer to any one of the values of P (the use of i and j as general
subscripts is a common, but arbitrary practice; any letter could be used;
the ones most frequently used however are i, j, k, and l).

Many of the models to be examined later use double subscripts. If, for
example, we use T to represent the number of trips or journeys made by
an individual, we can describe the trips made between area 1 and area 2
as T_{12}—the number of trips *from* area 1 *to* area 2. Similarly T_{23} would
describe the trips between area 2 and area 3. Or, using the general notation, T_{ij} represents the number of trips from area i to area j.

SUMMATION SIGNS

Much of the calculation involved in using models is addition. If there
are large numbers of subscripted variables in the model, the equations
describing the relationships between variables can become very large and
complex. In order to simplify formulae that involve large sets of numerical
data, the symbol Σ (capital Greek sigma, standing for S) is used. This is
simply a piece of mathematical shorthand which means "the sum of", but
experience shows that it is the use of Σ together with subscripts which
causes the greatest difficulties of comprehension for the non-numerate
student. As an understanding of the meaning and use of Σ is critical to the
discussion of models, we will spend some time explaining this important
symbol.

We will start with an example. If we return to our previous example of
the population of five areas, we know that the variable P_i has five values
(i.e. the subscript i has a range of values from 1 to 5). Assume that the
population of each of these areas is as shown below:

$$P_1 = 100 \qquad P_2 = 200 \qquad P_3 = 300$$
$$P_4 = 400 \qquad P_5 = 500$$

Total population, which we might call P_t, is found by summing the
populations of the five areas, i.e.

$$P_t = P_1 + P_2 + P_3 + P_4 + P_5.$$

We can represent the same thing much easier by using the summation size Σ:

$$P_t = \sum_{i=1}^{5} P_i$$

which simply says that total population P_t is the sum of all the values of P_i, starting with P_1 ($i = 1$) and going to P_5. The term

$$\sum_{i=1}^{5} P_i$$

means literally

$$P_1 + P_2 + P_3 + P_4 + P_5 .$$

The subscripts accompanying Σ do not have to refer to the whole range of the variable. For example,

$$\sum_{i=3}^{5} P_i$$

means the sum of all values of P_i starting at P_3 ($i = 3$) and going to P_5. In other words

$$\sum_{i=3}^{5} P_i = P_3 + P_4 + P_5.$$

We can now work out some actual totals using Σ and our example of population:

$$\sum_{i=1}^{5} P_i = P_1 + P_2 + P_3 + P_4 + P_5$$

$$= 100 + 200 + 300 + 400 + 500$$

$$= 1500.$$

Similarly,

$$\sum_{i=3}^{5} P_i = P_3 + P_4 + P_5$$

$$= 300 + 400 + 500$$

$$= 1200.$$

Once the meaning of the subscripts is clear it is not really necessary to write out the individual terms, so that we might simply say:

$$\sum_{i=2}^{4} P_i = 900.$$

(The answer was of course obtained by adding the values of P_i from P_2 to P_4.)

The general form of the summation sign is

$$\sum_{i=a}^{n}$$

which tells us that we are adding some variable that has a subscript i, and that we start with the subscript having the value a and add up all the variables up to and including the one having the subscript n.

Often, when the summation sign is meant to operate over all the values of a variable (i.e., in our example, from 1 to 5) the subscripts a and n are omitted, so that

$$\sum_{i}$$

means the sum of all the numbers having the subscript i.

We can also use the summation sign on variables which have double subscripts, and we will use another example to show how this might work.

Suppose that we have three towns, and we know that the number of journeys to work between each of the towns is as follows:

FROM	TO	NUMBER OF JOURNEYS
1	1	10
1	2	20
1	3	30
2	1	20
2	2	25
2	3	40
3	1	5
3	2	30
3	3	50

In fact this set of information can be shown in a much better way as a matrix, or table, the number in each "box" of the matrix representing the number of journeys between two towns:

FROM \ TO	1	2	3
1	10	20	30
2	20	25	40
3	5	30	50

If, as before, we use T_{ij} to represent the number of journeys between towns i and j, then from the table we can see that if $i = 1$ and $j = 3$, then $T_{ij} = 30$. Similarly, if $i = 3$ and $j = 2$, $T_{ij} = 30$.

Alternatively this can be expressed as

$$T_{13} = 30$$

$$T_{32} = 30$$

If we wanted to find the total number of trips *to* town 1 we need to add the trips which start and end in town 1, the trips from town 2 to town 1, and the trips from town 3 to town 1. In other words we want

$$T_{11} + T_{21} + T_{31}$$

or the sum of trips from all towns i to town 1. We know that the sum of trips from all towns with the subscript i to one town j can be represented as

$$\sum_{i=1}^{3} T_{ij}$$

so that the sum of trips from all towns to town 1 is

$$\sum_{i=1}^{3} T_{i1}.$$

Similarly the sum of trips from all towns to town 2 is

$$\sum_{i=1}^{3} T_{i2}$$

and the sum of trips from all towns to town 3 is

$$\sum_{i=1}^{3} T_{i3}.$$

If, therefore, we want to find the total number of trips made, we can add each of the three previous terms

$$\sum_{i=1}^{3} T_{i1} + \sum_{i=1}^{3} T_{i2} + \sum_{i=1}^{3} T_{i3}.$$

But the sum of trips from each town i to all towns j is

$$\sum_{j=1}^{3} T_{ij}$$

so that the total number of trips can be re-stated as

$$\sum_{i=1}^{3} \sum_{j=1}^{3} T_{ij}.$$

EXPONENTS

Exponents, or indices, represent another piece of mathematical short-hand. The summation sign provides a simplified way of writing additions; exponents provide a short method of writing multiple multiplications. Most people are familiar with the simple form of exponents; they know, for example, that 2×2 can be written as 2^2 and that 2^3 means $2 \times 2 \times 2$. However, the models to be discussed later will use two types of exponents which may be unfamiliar to the reader; or the meaning of which may not be very clear. They are (i) fractional exponents and (ii) negative exponents.

Fractional exponents may at first sight be confusing. Given that X^3 means three X's multiplied together, what does $X^{2 \cdot 5}$ mean? How exactly can we multiply $2\frac{1}{2}$ X's together? The answer is found by considering some of the basic properties of exponents. We know that 2^2 multiplied by 2^3 is 2^5 ($2^2 = 2 \times 2$; $2^3 = 2 \times 2 \times 2$; therefore, $2^2 \times 2^3 = 2 \times 2 \times 2 \times 2 \times 2 = 2^5$). In other words the multiplication of two numbers which have exponents is achieved by adding their exponents. In general we can say

$$X^a \times X^b = X^{a+b}.$$

Similarly, divison is carried out by subtracting the exponents, so that

$$2^5 \div 2^2 = 2^3.$$

We have seen that if a number is to be squared, its exponent is multiplied by two. If we want to find the square root of a number we divide its exponent by two. For example:

$$\sqrt{2^4} = 2^{4/2} = 2^2,$$

or

$$\sqrt{2^6} = 2^{6/2} = 2^3,$$

and

$$\sqrt[3]{2^6} = 2^{6/3} = 2^2.$$

The general form of this relationship is

$$\sqrt[b]{X^a} = X^{a/b}.$$

It is this latter relationship which gives a clue to the meaning of fractional exponents. In dividing exponent a by exponent b it is obviously possible to obtain a fraction. $X^{2 \cdot 5}$ is equal to $X^{5/2}$, which from the logic of the previous section means $\sqrt{X^5}$; $X^{1 \cdot 5}$ is equal to $X^{3/2}$ which is $\sqrt{X^3}$.

Negative exponents present no further complications. We know that we subtract the exponents of two numbers to be divided. Thus $X^4 \div X^2 = X^{4-2}$ or X^2. It is obvious that if the exponent of the divisor is greater than the exponent of the dividend, the result will be a negative exponent, as in the following example:

$$X^2 \div X^4 = X^{2-4} = X^{-2}.$$

We can easily demonstrate what this means by working through the equation in full:

$$\frac{X^2}{X^4} = \frac{X \times X}{X \times X \times X \times X} = \frac{1}{X \times X} = \frac{1}{X^2}.$$

Similarly

$$X^3 \div X^6 = X^{3-6} = X^{-3}$$

or

$$\frac{X \times X \times X}{X \times X \times X \times X \times X \times X} = \frac{1}{X \times X \times X} = \frac{1}{X^3}.$$

In general, therefore, we can say that

$$X^{-a} = \frac{1}{X^a}.$$

SOLVING EQUATIONS

Most of the following chapters include sections which manipulate equations in one way or another. The purpose of manipulating equations is to find the value of one of the variables in which we are interested. For example, in the expression

$$2A + 4B = 16$$

we might be interested in the value of A, and we would want to re-express the equation so that the value of A can be found directly, given the value of B. In this case we would rearrange the equation as follows:

$$A = 8 - 2B.$$

The rules for manipulating equations in this way are really quite simple, but experience suggests that many people forget them easily. A few examples will be provided as references for the work of later chapters.

If we start with a trivial equation,

$$A = A$$

and let b represent any other number, then it is obvious that

$$A + b = A + b$$

and

$$A - b = A - b$$

and

$$A \times b = A \times b$$

and

$$\frac{A}{b} = \frac{A}{b}$$

This demonstrates the four main principles on which the solution of equations is based: that the value, or "truth", of an equation is not altered if the same number is added to, or subtracted from, *both sides* of the equation, or if both sides are multiplied or divided by the same number.

This holds true for all equations, however complex, not only for the simple equality expressed above.

A few examples will demonstrate how the principles work:

1. $$A+9 = 16$$
   Subtract 9 from both sides: $$A = 7$$

2. $$A-9 = 16$$
   Add 9 to both sides: $$A = 25$$

3. $$5A = 15$$
   Divide each side by 5: $$A = 3$$

4. $$\frac{A}{4} = 10$$
   Multiply each side by 4: $$A = 40$$

5. $$5A+10 = 25$$
   Subtract 10 from each side: $$5A = 15$$
   Divide each side by 5: $$A = 3$$

When the equations become more complex, the solutions may be a little more difficult. Take the equation

$$5A+2cA+2dA = 10.$$

We can't in this example subtract anything from the left-hand side and leave A on its own. However, in the expression

$$5A+2cA+2dA$$

the symbol A is common to each of the terms, and therefore can be "factored out" of the equation, so that

$$5A+2cA+2dA = A(5+2c+2d)$$

The solution to the problem is then

$$A(5+2c+2d) = 10$$

$$A = \frac{10}{(5+2c+2d)}.$$

This concludes our introduction to the mathematical operations and symbols which are used in the models described later. The coverage has deliberately not been extensive or rigorous. The intention has been only to introduce the elements of mathematical language and operations which are necessary to understand the following discussion.

REFERENCES

The reader who wishes to take up any of the points raised in this chapter, or to revise his knowledge of mathematics as a general preliminary to using quantitative models, could usefully consult any of the following:

BASHAW, W. I. (1969) *Mathematics for Statistics*. John Wiley & Sons.

COYLE, R. G. (1971) *Mathematics for Business Decisions*. Nelson.

LEWIS, J. P. (1959) *An Introduction to Mathematics for Students of Economics*. Macmillan.

O'BRIAN, R. J. and GARCIA, G. G. (1971) *Mathematics for Economists and Social Scientists*. Macmillan.

CHAPTER 4

Linear Models

INTRODUCTION

It has been suggested in earlier chapters that mathematical models are based on relationships between the elements (variables) of a system.

Relationships between variables are often complex and difficult to identify. However, experience has shown that frequently such relationships are of a linear form (the term is explained fully below) or can be modified so that they can be approximated by a linear relationship. Models which are based on linear relationships are called linear models, and the purpose of this chapter is to explain the structure and significance of linear models, and to look at a few simple examples of their use.

The organisation of the chapter is as follows:

(i) Simple linear relationships.
(ii) Multiple-variable models.
(iii) Measuring the strength of linear relationships.
(iv) Problems and limitations.
(v) Examples of use.

SIMPLE LINEAR RELATIONSHIPS

Linear models are models in which the relationship between the variables of the model is expressed in a linear equation. Linear equations are so called because the variables change in direct proportion to each other, and when such a relationship between the variables is plotted on ordinary graph paper, it forms a straight line. The data shown in Table 4.1, for example, represents a linear relationship.

TABLE 4.1

No. in household	No. of journeys per household per day
1	4
2	6
3	8
4	10
5	12

If this data is plotted on a graph, the linear relationship becomes obvious, as shown in Fig. 4.1.

The relationship can also be expressed by an equation—a linear equation—of the form:

$$Y = a + b.X$$

where Y represents the number of journeys, and X represents the number of persons per household. The equation states that Y is related to X in a linear fashion: a and b are numerical constants which indicate the numerical relationship between changes in X and Y. Once the numerical constants are known, a predicted value of Y can be obtained for any given value of X.

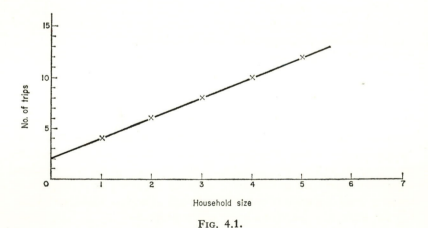

FIG. 4.1.

In the example quoted above, the equation which represents the data shown on the graph is:

$$Y = 2 + 2.X.$$

If we wanted to know the number of trips which would be produced by a household of 6 persons, all that is necessary is to substitute 6 into the equation in place of X, and to solve the equation for the value of Y. Thus

$$Y = 2 + 2.6$$
$$= 14.$$

The implication of using the equation in this manner is that the variable on the left-hand side of the equation *depends on* the value of the variable on the right-hand side, i.e. the number of journeys made depends on household size. Thus the variable Y is called the *dependent variable*, and variable X is known as the *independent variable*.

Linear models are useful and important not only because there are many relationships which are actually of a linear form, but also because linear equations often provide close approximations to complicated relationships which would otherwise be difficult to describe.

It is very rare for a linear equation to explain the relationship between two variables exactly. The first stage in developing a linear model is therefore that of fitting a straight line to a set of data consisting of sets of observations of the two variables X and Y. This can be done by using the statistical technique of linear regression. To illustrate the problem, let us consider the hypothetical set of data shown in Table 4.2 relating to journeys and household size.

Plotting the points corresponding to these 17 sets of observations, as in Fig. 4.2, it is obvious that although the points do not fall exactly on a straight line, they are reasonably close to the dashed line shown on the diagram. If, on the basis of this set of data, it is decided that a straight line will provide a fairly good description of the relationship between household size and the number of journeys made by households, the problem becomes one of finding the equation for the line which in some sense provides the best possible fit to the data, and which may therefore yield the best possible forecast.

It would, of course, be possible to fit a straight line to the data by eye. Because of the largely subjective nature of this method of curve-fitting,

TABLE 4.2

Observation no.	Household size	No. of journeys
1	1	4
2	1	5
3	2	5
4	2	6
5	3	6
6	3	7
7	3	9
8	4	9
9	4	11
10	5	13
11	5	12
12	5	11
13	6	12
14	6	13
15	6	14
16	7	14
17	7	16

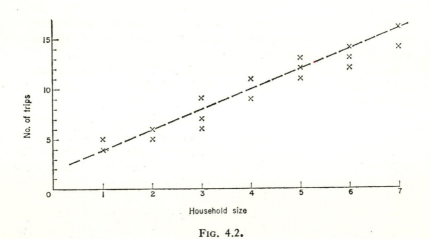

FIG. 4.2.

however, it is not recommended. The method which is almost universally used for fitting straight lines to numerical data is *the method of least squares*. The criterion used by the least-square method is that the line which is fitted to the data must *minimise the sum of the squares of the vertical deviations from the line to the actual points.*

The logic behind the least-squares approach may be explained by considering the last numerical example in more detail. If we refer to Fig. 4.3, the criterion of least squares requires that, for the line which is fitted to our set of data, the sum of the squares of the solid lines be a minimum.

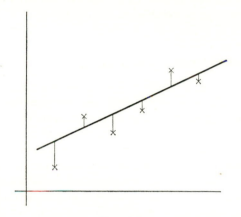

Fig. 4.3.

The tenth observation in the set of data describes a household of 5 people which makes 13 journeys per day. If we wanted to predict the number of journeys made by the tenth household, we could do so by either substituting $X = 5$ into the equation of the line, or by reading the predicted number of journeys directly from the diagram. As can be seen from the diagram, the vertical distance from the point representing the tenth observation is the difference between the actual number of journeys made, and the predicted number, and thus measures the error of the prediction.

The reason we want to minimise the sum of the square of the vertical deviations (or errors) and not just their sum is that some of the differences between the observed values of Y and the values on the line are positive while some are negative. If we considered only the sum of the deviations, it would be possible for this sum to be zero even though the deviations are quite large.

The method of calculating the values of *a* and *b* which give the "least-squares" line is shown in the Appendix at the end of the book. Although it is possible to calculate these values by hand, if large numbers of observations are to be dealt with, the calculations can become tedious, and there are many standard computer programs available which can be used to calculate the values quickly and easily. Once the equation of the line has been determined, it can be used for prediction simply by inserting future values of the independent variable into the equation.

MULTIPLE - VARIABLE MODELS

A particularly valuable feature of linear models is the fact that they can be used to describe relationships, not only between two variables, but between several variables. If two or more factors are thought to affect the dependent variable, the simple two-variable model (as illustrated above) must be extended to measure the influence of each factor acting in association with the other. Thus it might be suspected that the total number of journeys per household depends not only on household size, but also on the number of workers in the household and the number of cars owned by the household. This relationship could be described by a multiple-variable linear equation of the form:

$$Y = a + b.X_1 + c.X_2 + d.X_3$$

where Y is the number of journeys per household,

   X_1 is the number of persons per household,

   X_2 is the number of workers per household,

   X_3 is the number of cars owned by each household.

As before, the lower-case letters *a*, *b*, *c*, and *d* are numerical constants which describe by how much the dependent variable Y changes in relation to changes in the independent variables. If, for example, the values of the constants were:

$$a = 2; \ b = 0.75; \ c = 0.5; \ d = 2$$

the equation would be:

$$y = 2 + 0.75 . X_1 + 0.5 . X_2 + 2 . X_3.$$

If we then wanted to find Y, the number of journeys made, for a household of four people ($X_1 = 4$), all of whom are workers ($X_2 = 4$), and who own two cars ($X_3 = 2$), the model tells us that the family would make eleven journeys per day, as follows:

$$Y = 2 + 0.75 . (4) + 0.5 . (4) + 2 . (2)$$
$$= 2 + \quad 3 \quad + \quad 2 \quad + \quad 4$$
$$= 11.$$

If the linear equation includes three variables, the graph illustrating the relationship can be extended to three dimensions, but when more than three variables are included it becomes impossible to graphically represent the relationship. Nevertheless the principle behind the use of multiple-variable linear models is exactly the same as that behind the use of the simple two-variable model outlined above.

MEASURING THE STRENGTH OF LINEAR RELATIONSHIPS

It was suggested earlier that it is very rare for a linear equation to explain the changes in the dependent variable precisely, and it was shown how the technique of linear regression determines the equation which gives the "best" description of the changes in the dependent variable, i.e. the equation which keeps the difference between actual data and the values predicted by the equation to a minimum. The strength of the relationship between the actual and predicted values is measured by *the coefficient of correlation* (R). A value of 0 for the coefficient of correlation means that there is no linear relationship between the variables (i.e. if the observed values of the variables were plotted on a graph, they would not fall on, or near to, a straight line). Values of $+1$ or -1 indicate that there is a very strong linear relationship (perfect correlation), with all the variation in the dependent variable being accounted for by changes in the independent variables. The interpretation of values of other than 0 or ± 1 for the correlation coefficient is rather more difficult. Generally it may be said that a correlation coefficient of ± 0.8 or more indicates a strong relationship, while a coefficient of less than 0.8 represents a rather weak relationship.

Another useful measure of the strength of the linear relationship between variables is the coefficient of determination. This is the square of the correlation coefficient (R^2), and it means that $100 \times R^2$ per cent of the variation of the dependent variable is accounted for by changes in the independent variable. Thus with a correlation coefficient of 1, 100×1^2, or 100% of the variation in the dependent variable is accounted for by changes in the independent variable. With a coefficient of 0.9, then 100×0.9^2, or 81% of the total variation is accounted for; a coefficient of 0.8 means that 64% of the variation in the dependent variable is accounted for by changes in the independent variable.

The method of calculation of the correlation coefficient is shown in the Appendix. As with the constants in a regression equation, the calculation can be laborious if large numbers of observations are included, and a computer program will usually be used.

PROBLEMS AND LIMITATIONS

The main limitation on the use of linear models is the fact that many of the relationships with which planners are concerned may not be linear in form. It may be possible to transform the variables into linear form (e.g. by using the logarithmic values of the variables), but it is not always easy to determine whether the relationship is linear or not. This situation is complicated by the fact that a low correlation coefficient, although it indicates no strong *linear* relationship, does not necessarily mean that there is *no* significant relationship between the variables. There may, for example, be a strong curvilinear relationship, as indicated in Fig. 4.4.

The real advantage of linear models, however, is that they are easy and cheap to use, because they are based on a widely used standard statistical technique. There are many computer programs with which the models can be operated both quickly and cheaply, thus enabling a wide range of factors to be included and tested for relevance. Moreover, whatever the limitations, they have been proved to work, in the sense that they have satisfactorily reproduced existing patterns of urban activities. Whether or not they will prove to be as successful in predicting future patterns can only be determined by the passage of time (the use of such models for forecasting does assume that the relationships between the variables will remain constant over time).

It is fairly obvious, however, that many relationships with which the planner is concerned are not of the simple linear kind implied by the use

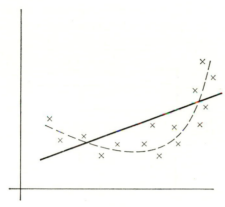

Fig. 4.4.

of such models. As our understanding of urban areas improves, and as our ability to represent that understanding in symbolic form improves, it can be expected that linear models will be discarded in favour of more realistic constructs. Until that happens it seems likely that the planner will continue to use such models as are available.

EXAMPLES OF USE

The purpose of this section is not to review operational models, although reference will be made to models which have been used in planning or research studies, so that the reader can follow up for himself the detailed application of the models described here. The objective here is to work through the structure of linear models using simplified examples, in order to demonstrate the principles on which they operate. Two examples have been chosen, one based on a simple (i.e. with only one independent variable) linear model, and the other based on a model using two independent variables. Both of the examples are based on work done by the

Leicester/Leicestershire Sub-regional Planning Team, as described in their published reports (Leicester City Council, 1969).

A flowchart indicating the general sequence of activities or calculations will be provided for each of the models to be examined in this and subsequent chapters. This is intended to help the reader to relate the detailed component parts of the calculation to the overall model structure. The flowchart for the linear models to be discussed now is shown in Fig. 4.5.

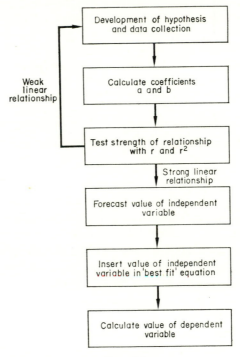

Fig. 4.5.

Obviously before collecting data to use in a model, the user must have some hypothesis about the nature and behaviour of the system in which he is interested. The models used here are models for distributing or allocating a regional growth of population to zones within the region, and are based on hypotheses first developed in model form by Hill (1965) and Lowry (1964). The proposition on which the models are based is that population change in an area is closely related to the change in employment opportunities. More precisely, they assume that, "Changes in each zone's share of all the (sub) region's jobs would go a long way to explain the changes in population; furthermore, that the population's response would tend to lag behind the priming effect of job changes" (Leicester City Council, 1969).

The assumption of a lagged response (with changes in population lagging behind employment) seems to be a reasonable one; it will obviously take time for people to become aware of new job opportunities, and to let this awareness affect their decisions as to where to live; a time lag is also necessary to allow the housing market to respond to the changing locational demands for housing.

The formal structure of the model can be expressed as:

$$\Delta P_{k(t/t+5)} = a + b\Delta E_{k(t-5/t)}$$

where ΔP_k is the population change in zone k,

ΔE_k is the change in total employment in zone k,

a and b are the parameters which describe by how much population changes for a given change in employment,

$(t/t+5)$ and $(t-5/t)$ are subscripts denoting five-year intervals of time (in other words, a five-year lag is being assumed).

The verbal equivalent of this formal model is: the population change in zone k during a five-year period (from time t to time $t+5$) is proportional to the change in total employment in the zone in the previous five-year period (from time $t-5$ to t); the exact nature of the proportional relationship is determined by the parameters a and b.

To test this relationship we need population and employment data for three points in time, times t, $t-5$, and $t-10$. The examples to be used in later chapters are based on a hypothetical urban area with three zones. However, more than three observations of population and data are needed to give a reliable estimate of the linear relationship between the variables. The data have therefore been disaggregated into six zones, as shown in Table 4.3. But our model is based on a hypothesised relationship between population change and employment change, so we need to work out the figures for change for each time-period (Table 4.4).

TABLE 4.3

Zone	Total employment			Total population		
	Time t	Time $t-5$	Time $t-10$	Time t	Time $t-5$	Time $t-10$
1 (1A)	1400	700	400	6500	3500	2500
2 (1B)	2600	1300	1000	12,500	8000	6000
3 (2A)	6500	3500	1750	28,000	19,000	9000
4 (2B)	1500	1000	900	7000	5000	4000
5 (3A)	14,000	8500	8000	17,500	11,000	10,000
6 (3B)	18,000	13,000	9000	23,500	16,000	12,000
Total	44,000	28,000	21,050	95,000	62,500	43,500

TABLE 4.4

Zone	Total employment	Total population
	$t-10$ to $t-5$	$t-5$ to t
1	300	3000
2	300	4500
3	1750	9000
4	100	2000
5	500	6500
6	4000	7500

We now need to calculate the value of the coefficients a and b, and to test whether there is a strong linear relationship between population change and employment change. We will use the method described in the Appendix to calculate a and b. As shown in the Appendix we can calculate the values from the following equations:

$$b = \frac{n(\sum_i x_i y_i) - (\sum_i x_i)(\sum_i y_i)}{n(\sum_i x_i^2) - (\sum_i x_i)^2}$$

$$a = \frac{\sum_i y_i - b \sum_i x_i}{n}$$

where n is the number of observations, x is employment change, and y is population change.

Table 4.5 provides us with the necessary totals:

TABLE 4.5

x	y	x^2	xy
300	3000	90,000	900,000
300	4500	90,000	1,350,000
1750	9000	3,062,500	15,750,000
100	2000	10,000	200,000
500	6500	250,000	3,250,000
4000	7500	16,000,000	30,000,000
$\Sigma x_i = 6950$	$\Sigma y_i = 32{,}500$	$\Sigma x_i{}^2 = 19{,}502{,}500$	$\Sigma x_i y_i = 51{,}450{,}000$

This gives $n = 6$, $\Sigma x_i = 6950$, $\Sigma y_i = 32{,}500$, $\Sigma x_i^2 = 19{,}502{,}500$, $\Sigma x_i y_i = 51{,}450{,}000$.

Substituting these values into the equation for b we get

$$b = \frac{6(51{,}450{,}000) - (6950)(32{,}500)}{6(19{,}502{,}500) - (6950)^2} = 1\cdot2.$$

Substituting this value for b into the equation for a we get

$$a = \frac{32{,}500 - 1\cdot2(6950)}{6} = 4026$$

and we can therefore write the equation representing the relationship between employment change and population change as:

$$\Delta P = 4026 + 1\cdot2\Delta E.$$

The correlation coefficient for this equation (calculated by a computer program) is $0\cdot67$. The relationship is therefore a weak one, and one would not therefore have much confidence in using it for prediction (in practice one would not in any case have a great deal of confidence in a relationship derived from only six observations).

The Leicester/Leicestershire Team tried to improve the results of this simple model by recognising the more sophisticated relationship between changes in employment and population identified by Lowry (1964). In "Model of Metropolis", Lowry drew a distinction between "basic" employment (including manufacturing), which determines the location of population, and "service employment", which is generated by the level of population. The second version of the model therefore becomes:

$$\Delta P_{k(t/t+5)} = a + b\Delta B_{k(t-5/t)} + c\Delta S_{k(t-5/t)}$$

where B is basic employment and S is service employment.

To test this relationship, data is needed for basic and service employment at three points in time. The set of data in Table 4.6 was used to calculate the coefficients a, b and c.

TABLE 4.6

Zone	Δ Basic employment Time $t-10$ to $t-5$	Δ Service employment Time $t-10$ to $t-5$	Δ Population Time $t-5$ to t
1	300	0	3000
2	200	100	4500
3	700	1050	9000
4	50	50	2000
5	200	300	6500
6	1200	2800	7500

Because the calculation of the regression coefficients for two independent variables is lengthy, even with only six observations, a computer program was used. The values obtained are shown in the following equation:

$$\Delta P_{k(t/t+5)} = 3014 + 7 \cdot 4(\Delta B_{k(t-5/t)}) - 1 \cdot 2(\Delta S_{k(t-5/t)}).$$

The strength of the relationship as measured by the correlation coefficient, improves from 0·67 to 0·72, but this is still not a very high value. If one wanted to use the model for forecasting, however, the next step would be to obtain the values of the independent variables (ΔB and ΔS) and to insert these values into the equation to obtain the estimated value of the dependent variable, ΔP. If, for example, an estimate of population change in each zone was required for the period from time t to $(t+5)$, figures would be needed for changes in basic and service employment for the period from time $(t-5)$ to time t.

Table 4.7 shows the appropriate data, derived from the same data used in Table 4.3.

TABLE 4.7

Zone	Basic employment		Service employment		Δ Basic $(t-5)$ to t	Δ Service $(t-5)$ to t
	Time t	Time $(t-5)$	Time t	Time $(t-5)$		
1	1000	600	400	100	400	300
2	1800	1100	800	200	700	600
3	3000	1700	3500	1800	1300	1700
4	1000	800	500	200	200	300
5	6000	3600	8000	4900	2400	3100
6	6000	4800	12,000	8200	1200	3800

We can use this data to estimate the future change in population in each zone as follows:

$$\Delta P_1 = 3014 + 7{\cdot}4(400) \ -1{\cdot}2(300) \ = \ 5614$$

$$\Delta P_2 = 3014 + 7{\cdot}4(700) \ -1{\cdot}2(600) \ = \ 7474$$

$$\Delta P_3 = 3014 + 7{\cdot}4(1300) - 1{\cdot}2(1700) = 12{,}634$$

$$\Delta P_4 = 3014 + 7{\cdot}4(200) \ -1{\cdot}2(300) \ = \ 4134$$

$$\Delta P_5 = 3014 + 7{\cdot}4(2400) - 1{\cdot}2(3100) = 17{,}054$$

$$\Delta P_6 = 3014 + 7{\cdot}4(1200) - 1{\cdot}2(3800) = 10{,}348$$

Although this example gives an idea of the method and principle of developing and using linear models, there are in practice several additional problems involved in their use. The interested reader could usefully consult the works of Arnold (1969), Colenut (1968), Hill (1965), Siedman (1966), and Turner (1969, 1970) for a consideration of some of the problems involved in the operational use of linear models.

REFERENCES

ARNOLD, E. L. (1969) *Growth allocation models of land development.* Discussion Paper No. 7, Dept. of Town Planning, University College, London.
COLENUT, R. J. (1968) Building linear predictive models for urban planning. *Regional Studies*, vol. 2, pp. 139–143.
HILL, D. M. (1965) A growth allocation model for the Boston region. *Journal of the American Institute of Planners*, May.

C

LOWRY, I. S. (1964) *A Model of Metropolis*. The Rand Corporation No. R.M. 4125 R.C.

SIEDMAN, D. (1966) *The Construction of an Urban Growth Model*. Delaware Valley Regional Planning Commission, Report No. 1, Vol. A.

TURNER, C. G. (1969) *Hamburg: A study in multivariate analysis*. Discussion Paper No. 8, Dept. of Town Planning, University College, London.

TURNER, C. G. (1970) *Hamburg: The interpretation of regression analysis*. Discussion Paper No. 10, Dept. of Town Planning, University College, London.

CHAPTER 5

Gravity Models

INTRODUCTION

Gravity models have probably been used in planning and transport studies more than any other form of mathematical model. It is therefore particularly important that the reader should understand the principles on which they are based, and the ways in which they can be used. The organisation of the chapter is as follows:

  (i) Origin of gravity models.

 (ii) The modern form of the gravity model.

(iii) Gravity models as location models.

(iv) Problems and limitations.

 (v) Examples of use.

ORIGIN OF GRAVITY MODELS

The models described in Chapter 4 were based on a standard statistical technique which was applied to the analysis of parts of the urban system. Gravity models have been developed and adapted from relationships which were discovered in the field of the physical sciences, and applied to the social sciences. They have been used to analyse the interaction between various urban activities for several decades, and are so called because the gravity concept of human interaction is based on the Newtonian concept of gravity. Sir Isaac Newton's Law of Universal Gravitation states that: "Two bodies in the universe attract each other in proportion to the product of their masses, and inversely to the square of their distance apart." This can be written mathematically as:

$$F = \frac{GM_1M_2}{D^2}$$

where F = the force which each body exerts on the other,

M_1 and M_2 = the mass or size of the two bodies,

D = distance between the two bodies,

G = a constant, which is the pull or force of gravity.

In the applications of the gravity concept to the analysis of urban systems, the gravitational pull exerted by two bodies has been interpreted as the amount of interaction between two areas, and the mass of the bodies has been measured in terms of size or attractiveness of the areas. The earliest and simplest gravity models were based on the proposition that the amount of interaction between two areas is related directly to the size (or attraction) of the areas, and inversely to the distance separating the areas (the distance usually being raised to a power). This simple version of the gravity model can be expressed mathematically as:

$$I_{ij} = G\frac{P_iP_j}{d_{ij}^b} \tag{1}$$

where I_{ij} = the interaction between areas i and j,

P_i, P_j = the size of areas i and j,

d_{ij} = the distance between area i and j,

b = a power or exponent applied to the distance between the areas,

G = a constant, equivalent to the gravitational constant, which is empirically determined, and is used to relate the relationship to actual conditions.

The meaning and significance of this formulation of the gravity model can be explained by use of an example. A useful way of understanding the concepts of interaction embodied in the gravity model is to think in terms of the probability of interaction between two areas.

Let us consider a hypothetical urban region with three zones, and a total population, P, of 25,000. Assume also that the total number of trips per day, T, made by this population is 75,000. The interaction between the three zones of this urban area could be described in terms of the number of trips made between each pair of zones (i.e. between zones 1 and 2; 1 and 3; 2 and 1; 2 and 3; 3 and 1; 3 and 2; and the internal trips within zones 1, 2 and 3, i.e. those trips with both origin and destination in the same zone). The gravity model suggests that the amount of interaction between two areas varies directly with the size or attraction of the areas and inversely with the distance between them. If, for the moment, we ignore the effect of distance on interaction (i.e. we assume that no costs and no time are involved in making a trip from one area to another), the volume of trips going from any one zone, i, to any other zone, j, would be directly proportional to the possibility of a trip finding a suitable destination in zone j. The relative attraction of zone j (in terms of the desire of population from another zone to make trips to j) will be equal to the population of zone j, (P_j) divided by the total population of the region, P. That is, the proportion of journeys from any one zone which have their destination in zone j will be equal to the ratio P_j/P. Thus in our hypothetical urban region, if zone 3 has a population of 10,000 ($P_3 = 10,000$) compared with a total population of 25,000, the proportion of journeys made by an individual from any other zone to zone 3 will be 10,000/25,000 or 0·4 (40%).

Having calculated the *proportion* of trips going to zone j, it is easy to calculate the actual number of trips involved. The average number of journeys made by an individual in the region is T/P; if we represent this average number by K, then the actual number of journeys made to zone j by an individual living in zone i is represented by $K \times (P_j/P)$. If there are P_i individuals living in zone i, then the total number of trips made by individuals to zone j will be P_i times the number of trips made by an individual, that is:

$$T_{ij} = K\frac{P_iP_j}{P} \tag{2}$$

where T_{ij} represents the total number of trips made by individuals living in zone i which terminate in zone j.

Referring to our example, K, the average number of journeys made, is T/P

or 3. If we are interested in the interaction between zones 1 and 3 ($i = 1, j = 3$) and the value of P_1 is 6000, the value of T_{ij} can be found as follows:

$$T_{ij} = 3 \times \frac{6000 \times 10{,}000}{25{,}000} = 7200.$$

In a similar manner we could estimate the expected number of trips between each pair of zones in the region, so obtaining a description of the interaction between all the component parts of the urban area.

It is obvious that the hypothesis of interaction developed above is a gross oversimplification, because of the initial assumption that distance or cost have no effect on trip-making behaviour. The gravity model in fact suggests that as the distance between two zones increases, the amount of interaction between the zones decreases. Ignoring the effect of distance, the attraction of zone j for journeys from other zones was seen to be proportional to the size of the population in j, P_j, relative to the total population of the region. The greater the proportion of the region's population living in zone j, the greater the number of journeys ending in j. However, the effect of distance on interaction can counteract the size or attractiveness of a zone. Given the size of zone j, the amount of interaction between two zones i and j will decrease as the distance increases, so that the attraction of zone j, previously defined as P_j/P, needs to be redefined as follows:

$$\frac{P_j/P}{d_{ij}} \tag{3}$$

where d_{ij} is the distance between zones i and j. This formulation expresses within one equation the two concepts already described. As the value of P_j/P increases, the attraction of zone j increases; as the value of d_{ij} increases, the attraction of zone j decreases. However, empirical studies reported by Isard (1960) and Carrol and Bevis (1957) suggest that the effect of distance on interaction is not uniform, and that long distances have a greater *proportional* deterrence effect than short ones. This means that it is not sufficient to incorporate a simple measure of distance into the expression for the attractiveness of a zone. The solution which is suggested by empirical studies is to express the deterrence effect of distance by raising the simple measure of distance to some power. The attractiveness of a zone can therefore be defined as

$$\frac{P_j/P}{d_{ij}^b} \tag{4}$$

where b is an exponent or power of distance. The effect of the exponent is to give large distances a greater proportional deterrence than small distances. For example, if the distance between zones i and j is 2 (the units by which distance is measured are not important for this purpose), and the exponent, b, has a value of 2, the distance effect in the gravity model would be $2^2 = 4$. If d_{ij} is equal to 4, the measure used in the model is $4^2 = 16$. Therefore, although actual distance in the second example is only twice as large as in the first, the deterrence effect of distance used in the gravity model is four times as big. The question of what value to give to the exponent, b, is a difficult one that is decided during the calibration of the model, and the problems of calibration are discussed later.

Using our latest definition of the attractiveness of a zone (the probability that a journey starting in zone i will find a destination zone j):

$$\frac{P_j/P}{d_{ij}^b}$$

we can now substitute this definition into equation (2) to redefine the interaction between zones i and j as follows:

$$T_{ij} = \frac{K\dfrac{P_iP_j}{P}}{d_{ij}^b}. \tag{5}$$

This equation can be simplified because, in any given area, K and P are both constants, which can be represented by one constant term which we might call G. Substituting G into equation for K/P, we obtain:

$$T_{ij} = G\frac{P_iP_j}{d_{ij}^b} \tag{6}$$

which is the same as equation (1).

Equation (6) describes the actual pattern of trip volumes within an urban area as a function of the population of the component zones of the area and the distance between zones. However, equation (6) represents only the relationship between one zone and any other zone. It would also be useful if we could describe the interaction between one zone and *all* other zones. We can do this quite easily by applying equation (6) to every zone. For example we could work out the interaction of zone i with the first of the other zones (this would be T_{i1}). To this we could add the interaction of i with the second zone (T_{i2}), and third (T_{i3}) and so on up to the interaction of zone i with the last zone, $n(T_{in})$. By adding the values of each of these interactions we obtain:

$$T_{i1}+T_{i2}+T_{i3}+...+T_{in} = G\frac{P_iP_1}{d_{i1}^b}+G\frac{P_iP_2}{d_{i2}^b}+G\frac{P_iP_3}{d_{i3}^b}+...+G\frac{P_iP_n}{d_{in}^b}.$$

This lengthy expression can be expressed neatly by using summation signs (see Chapter 3):

$$\sum_{j=1}^{n} T_{ij} = G\sum_{j=1}^{n}\frac{P_iP_j}{d_{ij}^b}. \tag{7}$$

THE MODERN FORM OF THE GRAVITY MODEL

The simple form of the gravity model expressed in equation (6) has been adapted to take into account not only the size or attractive power of zones and the distance separating the zones, but also the competition of other zones. Experience with the early formulations of the gravity model showed that they tended to over-predict the volume of short trips in an area. This experience led to a re-statement of the gravity model, which can be generally described in the following terms: the amount of inter-action between two or more zones is directly proportional to the size (or attractive power) of the zones, and is inversely proportional to the distance between the zones *and the relative attraction of competing zones*. In symbolic terms this means that a balancing factor is introduced as the denominator of the gravity model to represent the competing attraction of other zones:

$$T_{ij} = \frac{G\dfrac{P_iP_j}{d_{ij}^b}}{G\dfrac{P_1}{d_{i1}^b}+G\dfrac{P_2}{d_{i2}^b}+G\dfrac{P_3}{d_{i3}^b}+...+G\dfrac{P_n}{d_{in}^b}}. \tag{8}$$

This equation, which is useful to show the way in which the structure of the model has developed, is cumbersome if it is to be used frequently. Fortunately it can be substantially simplified by the use of mathematical conventions. For example, the expression

$$G \frac{P_i P_j}{d_{ij}^b} \quad \text{means} \quad G \times P_i \times P_j \times \frac{1}{d_{ij}^b}.$$

However, as we showed in Chapter 3,

$$\frac{1}{d_{ij}^b} \quad \text{can be written as} \quad d_{ij}^{-b},$$

so that the expression

$$G \frac{P_i P_j}{d_{ij}^b}$$

can be rewritten as $GP_i P_j d_{ij}^{-b}$.

Equation (8) can therefore be written as:

$$T_{ij} = \frac{GP_i P_j d_{ij}^{-b}}{GP_1 d_{i1}^{-b} + GP_2 d_{i2}^{-b} + GP_3 d_{i3}^{-b} + \ldots + GP_n d_{in}^{-b}}. \tag{9}$$

This can be further reduced by the use of the summation sign (see Chapter 3), where

$$G \sum_{j=1}^{n} P_j d_{ij}^{-b}$$

means the sum of the individual terms $GP_1 d_{i1}^{-b}$ to $GP_n d_{in}^{-b}$. Equation (9) therefore becomes:

$$T_{ij} = \frac{GP_i P_j d_{ij}^{-b}}{G \sum_{j=1}^{n} P_j d_{ij}^{-b}}. \tag{10}$$

In equation (10), the constant term G is common to both parts of the fraction and can therefore be cancelled out. Equation (10) then becomes:

$$T_{ij} = \frac{P_i P_j d_{ij}^{-b}}{\sum_{j=1}^{n} P_j d_{ij}^{-b}}. \tag{11}$$

A useful way of interpreting equation (11)—and one which we will use to develop our practical examples at the end of the chapter—is to regard the term

$$\frac{P_j d_{ij}^{-b}}{\sum_{j=1}^{n} P_j d_{ij}^{-b}}$$

as representing the probability of interaction between any zone i and zone j, based on the attraction of j compared with the attraction of all other zones. The actual amount of interaction is obtained by multiplying the probability of interaction by the total activity in zone i, Pi.

It is possible to simplify equation (11) further by rewriting the denominator of the equation. In the same way that we re-expressed

$$\frac{1}{d_{ij}^b} \quad \text{as} \quad d_{ij}^{-b}$$

so the expression

$$\frac{1}{\sum_{j=1}^{n} P_j d_{ij}^{-b}}$$

can be written as

$$(\sum_{j=1}^{n} P_j d_{ij}^{-b})^{-1}.$$

If we call this term A_i, we can write the gravity model formula much more simply as:

$$T_{ij} = P_i A_i P_j d_{ij}^{-b}. \tag{12}$$

In this equation, the probability of interaction between i and j is represented by $A_i P_j d_{ij}^{-b}$. The equation is usually written as:

$$T_{ij} = O_i A_i D_j d_{ij}^{-b} \tag{13}$$

where T_{ij} = the number of trips between zones i and j,

O_i = the number of trips originating in zone i,

D_j = measure of attraction of zone j.

GRAVITY MODELS AS LOCATION MODELS

The discussion so far has been in terms of using gravity models to describe interactions between zones. A very useful feature of gravity models, however, is their ability to provide estimates of activity by location—in other words they can be used as activity-location models, as well as interaction models. Equation (14), for example, can be used to allocate workers to zones of residence, or expenditure to shopping centres. If we think of using a gravity model to describe the flows of expenditure between a number of zones and shopping centres, where C_{ij} is the flow of expenditure from zone i to shopping centre j, we can imagine a matrix of expenditure flows as shown in Table 5.1.

TABLE 5.1. EXPENDITURE FLOWS BETWEEN ZONES AND SHOPPING CENTRES

From zone	To centre			Total
	1	2	3	
1	100	70	130	300
2	50	70	100	220
3	150	100	120	370
Total	300	240	350	890

If we take any one of the shopping centres, say centre 3, we can extract from the matrix of expenditure flows the expenditure from each zone to centre 3; thus from zone 1 to centre 3, 130 units; from zone 2 to centre 3, 100 units; from zone 3 to centre 3, 120 units. It is therefore possible to obtain an estimate of the total sales in centre 3 by summing the flows of expenditure from all three zones to centre 3. This can be expressed in symbols as follows:

$$S_3 = C_{13} + C_{23} + C_{33} = \sum_{i=1}^{3} C_{i3}$$

where S_3 is sales in centre 3,

and $\sum_{i=1}^{3} C_{i3}$ is the sum of the expenditure flows from all zones to centre 3.

Similarly if we were to develop a model which described the flows between place of employment and place of residence, it could be used to describe the location of population by summing the flows from all employment zones to each zone of residence, so that:

$$P_j = T_{1j} + T_{2j} + T_{3j} = \sum_{i=1}^{3} T_{ij}$$

where P_i = workers resident in zone j,

and $\sum\limits_{i=1}^{3} T_{ij}$ = the sum of the flows of workers from all zones of work-

place to one zone of residence, j.

Examples of both these kinds of use will be given later.

PROBLEMS AND LIMITATIONS

Various forms of the gravity model have now been in use for several years, and a substantial amount of practical experience has been obtained in their operation. There are many detailed problems of application, some of which are specifically related to particular versions of the model. As this chapter has only been concerned with a general formulation of the gravity method, the consideration of problems associated with the use of gravity models will be restricted to general problems. Reference will be made later to sources of information on more detailed problems relating to specific applications. The discussion will be organised around the following topics: absence of a sound theoretical base; the need for disaggregation; the form of the distance function; the importance of the zoning system; the problem of calibration.

Absence of a sound theoretical base

Perhaps the most fundamental criticism of gravity models is that they are not based on a theory of urban system behaviour. They are based on an analogy between the physical and social sciences which many people do not accept. Schneider (1959), for example, states: "There is no real kinship between a gravitational field and a trip generating system. . . . The theoretical supports on which the gravity method rests appear to be these: an interchange between two regions is clearly a descending function of the distance between them, and inverse proportion descends with engaging convenience. These are by no means contemptible grounds, but neither are they satisfactory. The cardinal failure of the gravity model is that it is not explanatory and does not really try to be. If it were an adequate predictor of interchange volumes . . . it would still only be a specific answer to a very special problem."

It is true that Wilson (1969a) has developed a theoretical explanation of the gravity model using information theory and entropy maximising methods, and has therefore partly reduced the force of this argument. It remains true, however, that there is still no adequate explanation of the gravity model in behavioural terms, so that it is difficult to see exactly what the proposition of the gravity formulation really means in terms of human behaviour. In other words we can conclude, as we did with linear regression models, that although they may *describe* interaction and activity patterns satisfactorily, they do not *explain* them. They look not at what is happening, but at the result of what has happened, summarising data to describe the present situation. J. Parry Lewis has described the dangers of using models which describe but do not explain, as follows: "The existing trip pattern reflects a long historical interaction of many forces, of decisions by shopkeepers where to put shops, as well as by planners of where to allow them; of decisions by people of where to live; by land owners of what land they will sell; of speculative builders of when and where they would develop, and so on. To use the observed parameters derived from a study of the pattern which has emerged from this set of interacting forces as a basis for predicting what will happen when a new shopping centre opens (but all else remains unchanged) or a new settlement created, is asking for trouble, for the extent to which the parametric values depend on the various forces is unmeasured" (J. Parry Lewis, 1970). This is perhaps an overstatement of the criticism: while it is undoubtedly true that the simple structure, with a few parameters, of both gravity and linear models does not enable the planner to identify the complex chain of cause and effect which gives rise to urban activity patterns, nevertheless it does seem that many of the patterns of behaviour which are summarised by the parameters of these models may be expected to remain more or less stable over the short (and perhaps the medium) term. The fact remains that these models, inadequate though they undoubtedly are, are amongst the best that we currently have, and do give partial answers to some of the questions the planner needs to ask. If the limitations of these answers are borne in mind, they can help to improve our understanding of the urban system's behaviour, and our ability to forecast and plan more effectively.

Disaggregation of gravity models

It is obvious from the derivation of the gravity model provided above, that the model is designed to account for the behaviour of large groups of people. It rests on the assumption that the behaviour of large groups of people is predictable on the basis of mathematical probability, because the idiosyncrasies of individuals or small groups tend to be cancelled out. On the other hand, we would expect that disaggregation of the models to take into account differentials in socio-economic characteristics and trip purpose would result in substantial improvements in their descriptive and forecasting ability. It is fairly obvious, for example, that trip-making behaviour is likely to vary according to trip purpose—people's willingness to travel to work is different from their willingness to undertake journeys for shopping.

Similarly in using gravity models as residential location models, Wilson (1969b) has suggested that, in particular, people seek houses they can afford. This has led Cripps (1968, 1971) to consider disaggregating these models to take account of:

(a) income groups in the population,
(b) wage levels in different locations,
(c) the existence of different types of house by location,
(d) the prices of each type of house by location,
(e) the possibility that different income groups may choose to spend different amounts on transport to work.

In addition to conflicting with the basic assumption about large-group behaviour, disaggregation increases the data requirements alarmingly. The results of the research by Cripps and his team will be of great interest and may help to resolve this conflict.

The distance function

Many of the practical and conceptual difficulties associated with the use of gravity models are related to the distance function which plays such an important part in the model formulation. The simple derivation of the gravity model used above suggested that the impedance effect of distance on the interaction between two areas is a power function—to be precise, a power function of distance. In fact there has been considerable discussion about the most appropriate variable for the measurement of impedance, while the large amount of practical experience which has been obtained suggests that a simple form of exponent is inadequate. We will discuss each of these problems in turn.

(a) In the earliest empirical tests of the gravity model, distance was used as the impedance variable. It is apparent, however, that pure distance is not a sufficiently accurate measure of the effects of spatial separation. Empirical evidence suggests that time is a more significant and critical variable than distance in its effect on trip-making behaviour. Most recent studies using the gravity model have incorporated some function of travel time rather than distance. The most recent developments, however (Wilson, 1969c), suggest that the most relevant variable is cost, but this raises problems of measurement.

(b) It has long been recognised that the exponent to be applied to the time/distance factor needs to be varied for different trip purposes—a reflection of the already observed fact that individuals are not willing to travel the same distance for all types of trips. There is much evidence to suggest that not only must the exponent vary with trip purpose, but also with distance itself. Studies have shown that a constant exponent is not capable of adequately reproducing interaction patterns over both short and long distances. This has led several people to suggest that the exponent to be applied should in fact vary with distance. Tanner, for example (Tanner, 1961), has suggested that instead of d_{ij}^{-b} a function of the form $e^{Lt} \times t^m$ should be used where t is the interzonal travel time or cost, L and m are constants to be determined empirically, and e is the exponential function with the value 2·71828. Similarly, Wilson (1969a) has suggested a function of the form $e^{-\beta t}$ where β is a constant to be determined empirically. In both of these functions, the fact that the interzonal travel time is included in the exponent means that the exponent varies as distance varies. This takes account of the fact that the friction against movement might be expected to be greater within an urban area than that caused by an equal distance in the less densely developed space between two such areas, and that an extra unit of time/distance added to a long movement is of less importance than an extra unit added to a short unit.

Zoning problems

The use of spatial interaction and location models implies that the area under study has been divided into component parts or zones. In practice zoning systems are usually fairly arbitrary, although the definition of zones is critical to model performance. Cripps (1968), for example, points out that if we are trying to describe inter-urban interaction, we will not have a very good model if a large proportion of the interaction actually takes place within the zones. The problems which are inherent in the definition of zones have been outlined by Broadbent (1969). He suggests that small zones are necessary to optimise locating the zone centroid (the hypothetical point which is taken as the origin and destination of interaction), and for the definition of spatial distributions and interaction (the point made by Cripps). In conflict with these requirements, large zones are needed to optimise accuracy of measurement and forecasting of zonal variables, conditions necessary for the application of statistical models where validity depends on having large numbers, data collection time and accurate measurement of intrazonal distance. Cripps (*op. cit.*) suggests that large zones are also necessary for economy in computation.

Problems of calibration

We have already seen (in Chapter 2) that calibration is the process of finding the values of the parameters in the model which provide the "best fit" between the model's performance and the behaviour of the real-world system. We also saw in Chapter 4, the techniques which have been developed to obtain the values of the parameters in linear models.

It may in some cases be possible to carry out linear transformations of the gravity model formula, and then use the same kinds of techniques as used for linear models. This is only possible, of course, if there is an adequate source of data on inter-zonal movements. The gravity model can be transformed to a linear equation by using logarithmic values: by finding the values of the constants in the linear equation, the value of the parameter *b* can be found. It is more usual, however, to carry out a trial-and-error process of running the model several times with different parameter values, and selecting the value which provides the best fit.

This still leaves the problem of how to decide which is the best fit. Perhaps the most obvious solution is to compare the predicted population and employment totals in each zone with the actual totals. The goodness of fit (of predicted to actual totals) can then be tested by statistical measure, such as the correlation coefficient. However, because the model is of interaction, as well as location, it is important to ensure that the process of calibration is based on the flows between zones. Batty (1970) and Cordey Hayes (1968) emphasise that if the model is calibrated only by comparing predicted and actual settlement patterns, "bogus" or "false" calibration is probable, i.e. the settlement pattern may be adequately reproduced, but the representation of interaction (journeys to work, or journeys to service centres) is completely false. Batty in particular suggests that the amount of travel in the system, as measured by the mean trip length (i.e. the average length of all trips made in the system) is a much more accurate measure of the model's predictive ability, and this has been widely used in calibration.

EXAMPLES OF USE

There are many different types of model based on the gravity concept. It is not possible, or even necessary, to examine all of them. However, a range of gravity models will be examined so that the reader can obtain some idea of the variety of forms which have been developed from the basic principle. This section will examine the following models:

   (i) Hansen's gravity/potential model.

  (ii) Single-constrained gravity model for locating retail trade.

 (iii) Double-constrained gravity model for trip distribution.

(i) Hansen's gravity/potential model

One of the earliest examples of the use of gravity-type models in a planning situation was the model developed by W. G. Hansen (Hansen, 1959). Hansen's model is a location model, which is designed to predict the location of population. It is based on the assumption that accessibility to employment is the major factor in determining the location of population. It is not really a gravity model because it is not based on the interaction between zones. It is perhaps more properly described as a "potential" model, because it is concerned with the "potential interaction" or relative accessibility of zones.

Hansen suggested that the relationship between population location and employment could be expressed in terms of an Accessibility Index, which defines for each zone its accessibility to employment. The accessibility index is calculated as follows:

$$A_{ij} = \frac{E_j}{d_{ij}^b}$$

where A_{ij} is the accessibility index of zone i in relation to zone j,

   E_j is total employment in j,

   d_{ij} is the distance between i and j,

   b is an exponent or power of d_{ij}.

This is the expression for the accessibility of zone i in relation to one zone j. The overall index for zone i is the sum of all the individual indices, so that

$$A_i = \sum_j \frac{E_j}{d_{ij}^b}.$$

Hansen also recognised that, in addition to accessibility, one of the major factors determining how much population will be attracted to a given area is the amount of vacant land that is suitable for residential use. He called this the "holding capacity" of a zone, and suggested that the two influences of accessibility and holding capacity could be combined by calculating an index of "development potential", obtained by multiplying the accessibility index by the holding capacity. The development potential of a zone, D_i, is therefore:

$$D_i = A_i H_i,$$

where H_i is the holding capacity of zone i. The development potential can be thought of as a measure of the attractiveness of each zone, based on access to employment and the amount of suitable residential land. Population is allocated to zones on the basis of the relative development potential of each of the zones, i.e. the development potential of each zone divided by the total potential of all zones:

$$\frac{A_i H_i}{\sum_i A_i H_i}.$$

In other words, Hansen suggested that the share of total population growth (which must be provided for the model) which will be obtained by any one zone is related to how attractive that zone is in relation to all the competing zones. If the total growth in population is G_t, then the amount of that growth going to any zone i will be:

$$G_i = G_t \frac{(A_i H_i)}{\left(\sum_i A_i H_i\right)} \quad \text{or} \quad G_t \frac{D_i}{\sum_i D_i}$$

where $D_i = A_i H_i$.

This provides a tool for allocating population which is relatively easy to use. It can be used to test the effects of different policy assumptions by specifying alternative distributions of employment, alternative journey times (reflecting different road proposals) and different holding capacities (representing different density or locational constraints). It is perhaps an appropriate device where a rapid and fairly crude assessment of the likely distribution of population is required.

Figure 5.1 is a flowchart showing the sequence of calculations for the Hansen model, and has been used for the following numerical example. Tables 5.2 and 5.3 show the data which will be used for all the remaining examples, based on an urban area with three zones.

TABLE 5.2

Zone no.	Basic employment	Service employment	Total employment	Total population	Holding capacity (acres)
1	2800	1200	4000	19,000	100
2	4000	4000	8000	35,000	125
3	12,000	20,000	32,000	41,000	100
Total	18,800	25,200	44,000	95,000	325

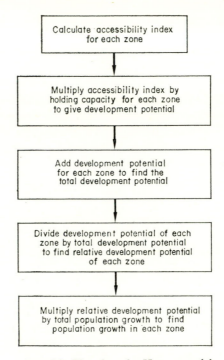

FIG. 5.1. Flowchart for Hansen model.

TABLE 5.3 DISTANCE/TRAVEL TIME MATRIX

To j From i	$j = 1$	$j = 2$	$j = 3$
$i = 1$	2	8	6
$i = 2$	8	3	4
$i = 3$	6	4	3

An exponent on distance of 2 is assumed to have been found from calibration.

The distance or travel time matrix represents the spatial separation of the zones—the time or distance taken to travel from the assumed centre of one zone to the centres of the others. Rather than use the models purely for forecasting, the procedure we will adopt from now on is to try to get the models to reproduce the known distribution of activities. All of the models require future employment (by location) as an input; we will input the existing figure of employment, and see whether the model can predict the correct (i.e. the *known*) location of population. From the flow diagram, the first step is to calculate the accessibility index for each zone:

$$A_{ij} = \frac{E_j}{d_{ij}^b}.$$

TABLE 5.4. CALCULATION OF A_{ij}

Zone	$j = 1$	$j = 2$	$j = 3$	$\sum_j A_{ij}$
$i = 1$	$\dfrac{4000}{2^2} = 1000$	$\dfrac{8000}{8^2} = 125$	$\dfrac{32{,}000}{6^2} = 888 \cdot 89$	2014
$i = 2$	$\dfrac{4000}{8^2} = 62 \cdot 5$	$\dfrac{8000}{3^2} = 888 \cdot 89$	$\dfrac{32{,}000}{4^2} = 2000$	2951
$i = 3$	$\dfrac{4000}{6^2} = 111 \cdot 1$	$\dfrac{8000}{4^2} = 500$	$\dfrac{32{,}000}{3^2} = 3555 \cdot 56$	4167

The fourth column,

$$\sum_j A_{ij},$$

is the accessibility index for zone i in relation to all other zones, i.e. $A_{i1} + A_{i2} + A_{i3}$. We can see, therefore, that:

$$A_1 = 2014$$
$$A_2 = 2951$$
$$A_3 = 4167$$

The next steps from the flow diagram are to calculate the development potential of each zone, and to find the total development potential. We have defined the development potential as $A_i H_i$, therefore we need to multiply each value of A_i by the appropriate holding capacity.

TABLE 5.5. DEVELOPMENT POTENTIALS

Zone	A_i	H_i	$D_i = A_i H_i$
1	2014	100	201,400
2	2951	125	368,924
3	4167	100	416,700

$$\sum_i D_i = 987,024$$

Next we need to calculate the relative development potential of each zone, i.e. its "attractiveness" compared to the total "attractiveness" of all other zones.

TABLE 5.6. RELATIVE DEVELOPMENT POTENTIAL

Zone	D_i	$D_i \div \sum_i D_i$
1	201,400	0·204
2	368,924	0·374
3	416,700	0·422
Total	987,024	1·000

Notice that the sum of the relative development potentials for each zone is 1. This must be the case, for all that the model is doing is allocating to each zone a proportion of the total development potential.

If we had an estimate of total growth in population, we could now calculate the share of that total which we could expect to go to each zone. In other words, we could allocate the total population growth to zones. Remember that what we are trying to do in the example is to get the model to reproduce a known situation. We know what the actual distribution of population is; what we are doing is seeing what the model predicts, so that we can compare this with the actual distribution. We know from our original data that the total population is 95,000 ($G_t = 95,000$) so that we can calculate the model's estimate of population in each zone:

$$G_i = G_t \frac{D_i}{\sum_i D_i} \cdot$$

TABLE 5.7. PREDICTED POPULATION GROWTH, G_i

Zone	$D_i \div \sum_i D_i$	$G_i = G_t \times (D_i \div \sum_i D_i)$
1	0·204	19,384
2	0·374	35,510
3	0·422	40,106
Total	1·000	95,000

We can now directly compare the model's predicted distribution of population with the actual distribution:

TABLE 5.8

Zone	Predicted population	Actual population	Difference
1	19,384	19,000	+384
2	35,510	35,000	+510
3	40,106	41,000	−894
Total	95,000	95,000	0

It is obvious that the model has reproduced the distribution of population very closely—remarkably well for a hypothetical example. The correlation between actual and predicted population is in fact 0·999.

If the model were to be used for forecasting, the actual population distribution would not be known (at least, not until the end of the forecast period), and the model would be operated with the predicted employment and the known holding capacities and travel times.

(ii) *Single-constrained gravity model for locating retail trade*

We have already seen briefly how the gravity model can be used to allocate activity to zones. This example uses what is sometimes known as the single-constrained gravity model to allocate consumer expenditure to retail centres. The reason for describing it as a single-constrained model is that the model is designed so that it meets the condition—or constraint—that

$$\sum_j T_{ij} = O_i.$$

In other words, if the trips from each zone of origin i to all other zones j are added, the total will be equal to the number of origins from each zone which were used as input into the model, O_i. On the other hand, if the model is used in a situation where both origins and destinations (O_i and D_j) are known, it will not be able to reproduce the known values of D_j, i.e.

$$\sum_i T_{ij} \neq D_j$$

or, if the trips from all zones of origin to each zone of destination are added, they will not be equal to the known destinations, D_j.

However, the model is a useful one in situations where the values of D_j (the predicted destinations) are not known. It can then be used to forecast or estimate these destinations. In the following example, the model is used to describe flows of expenditure rather than flows of people, but the form of the model is the same.

The model to be used is similar to the one developed by Lakshmanan and Hansen (1965) and has been widely used in planning studies in this country. The model describes expenditure flows between residential zones and shopping centres, and estimates sales in each centre by summing the flows of expenditure from all zones to each centre in turn. The model states that the sales, or retail turnover of a centre, is directly proportional to the size or attractiveness of the centre, and inversely proportional to the distance from residential zones, and to the competition from other centres. Formally, the model is similar to the gravity model described in equation (13),

$$S_{ij} = C_i A_i F_j^a d_{ij}^{-b}$$

where S_{ij} = expenditure from residential zone i to shopping centre j,

C_i = total expenditure in residential zone i,

F_i = size or attraction of shopping centre j,

$A_i = (\sum_j F_j d_{ij}^{-b})^{-1}$,

d_{ij} = distance from residential zone i to shopping centre j,

a and b are exponents.

The total sales in a shopping centre are therefore found by obtaining the sum of expenditure flows from all residential zones to that centre:

$$S_j = \sum_i C_i A_i F_j^a d_{ij}^{-b} = \sum_i S_{ij}.$$

The only difference from equation (13) (apart from the different symbols) is the addition of an exponent, a, to the attractiveness of each centre. This has been found to be necessary in most shopping studies, because large centres attract proportionately more trade than their size alone would indicate. This model needs data on expenditure and floorspace, as well as the time/distance matrix already provided. We will use the following data, keeping to our three-zone example, and assuming that each zone has one shopping centre.

TABLE 5.9

Expenditure in zone i (£)	Attraction (floorspace) (sq. ft.)
1,900,000	24,000
3,500,000	80,000
4,100,000	400,000

Assume also that $a = 1$ and $b = 2$.

The flowchart for the model is shown in Fig. 5.2.

The first two steps are necessary to be able to calculate the probability of interaction between each pair of zones, as represented by the term:

$$A_i F_j^a d_{ij}^{-b}.$$

First, therefore, we need to calculate the attraction of each centre, divided by the distance between the centre and the residential zones, and then obtain the total, $\sum_j F_j^a d_{ij}^{-b}$, for each residential zone (Table 5.10).

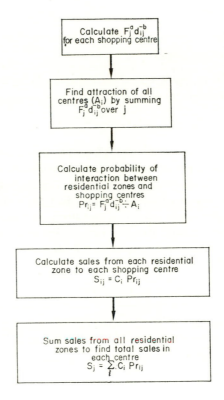

Fig. 5.2. Flowchart for retail trade location model.

Notice that we have calculated

$$A_i \quad \left(\text{i.e.} \sum_j F_j^a d_{ij}^{-b}\right)$$

in the previous step, and remember that for each residential zone i this term means

$$F_1^a d_{i1}^{-b} + F_2^a d_{i2}^{-b} + F_3^a d_{i3}^{-b}.$$

TABLE 5.10. $F_j^1 d_{ij}^{-2}$

i \ j	$j = 1$	$j = 2$	$j = 3$	$A_i = \sum\limits_j F_j^1 d_{ij}^{-2}$
$i = 1$	$\dfrac{24,000}{2^2} = 6000$	$\dfrac{8000}{8^2} = 125$	$\dfrac{400,000}{6^2} = 11,111 \cdot 11$	$17,236 \cdot 11$
$i = 2$	$\dfrac{24,000}{8^2} = 375$	$\dfrac{80,000}{3^2} = 8888 \cdot 89$	$\dfrac{400,000}{4^2} = 25,000$	$34,263 \cdot 89$
$i = 3$	$\dfrac{24,000}{6^2} = 666 \cdot 67$	$\dfrac{80,000}{4^2} = 5000$	$\dfrac{400,000}{3^2} = 44,444 \cdot 44$	$50,111 \cdot 11$

We can now calculate the probability of interaction, Pr_{ij}, between each pair of zones, as follows:

$$Pr_{ij} = A_i F_j^a d_{ij}^{-b} = \frac{F_j d_{ij}^{-b}}{\sum\limits_j F_j^a d_{ij}^{-b}}.$$

TABLE 5.11. $Pr_{ij} = F_j^1 d_{ij}^{-2} / (\sum\limits_j F_j^1 d_{ij}^{-2})$

i \ j	$j = 1$	$j = 2$	$j = 3$
$i = 1$	$\dfrac{6000}{17,236 \cdot 11} = 0 \cdot 35$	$\dfrac{125}{17,236 \cdot 11} = 0 \cdot 01$	$\dfrac{11,111 \cdot 11}{17,236 \cdot 11} = 0 \cdot 64$
$i = 2$	$\dfrac{375}{34,263 \cdot 89} = 0 \cdot 01$	$\dfrac{8888 \cdot 89}{34,263 \cdot 89} = 0 \cdot 26$	$\dfrac{25,000}{34,263 \cdot 89} = 0 \cdot 73$
$i = 3$	$\dfrac{666.67}{50,111 \cdot 11} = 0 \cdot 01$	$\dfrac{5000}{50,111 \cdot 11} = 0 \cdot 1$	$\dfrac{44,444 \cdot 44}{50,111 \cdot 11} = 0 \cdot 89$

Now we can calculate the expenditure from each zone to each centre:

$$S_{ij} = C_i Pr_{ij}.$$

$$S_{11} = C_1 Pr_{11} = 1,900,000 \times 0 \cdot 35 = 665,000$$
$$S_{12} = C_1 Pr_{12} = 1,900,000 \times 0 \cdot 01 = 19,000$$
$$S_{13} = C_1 Pr_{13} = 1,900,000 \times 0.64 = 1,216,000$$

$$S_{21} = C_2 Pr_{21} = 3,500,000 \times 0\cdot01 = \quad 35,000$$

$$S_{22} = C_2 Pr_{22} = 3,500,000 \times 0\cdot26 = \quad 910,000$$

$$S_{23} = C_2 Pr_{23} = 3,500,000 \times 0\cdot73 = 2,555,000$$

$$S_{31} = C_3 Pr_{31} = 4,100,000 \times 0\cdot01 = \quad 41,000$$

$$S_{32} = C_3 Pr_{32} = 4,100,000 \times 0\cdot1 \; = \quad 410,000$$

$$S_{33} = C_3 Pr_{33} = 4,100,000 \times 0\cdot89 = 3,649,000$$

If we present these results in tabular form, we can easily total the flows of expenditure from each zone to each centre:

TABLE 5.12. S_{ij}

i \ j	$j = 1$	$j = 2$	$j = 3$	Total
$i = 1$	665,000	19,000	1,216,000	1,900,000
$i = 2$	35,000	910,000	2,555,000	3,500,000
$i = 3$	41,000	410,000	3,649,000	4,100,000
Total	741,000	1,339,000	7,420,000	9,500,000

Since we know that

$$S_j = \sum_i S_{ij}$$

we can easily see that the total sales, S_j, of each centre are:

$$S_1 = S_{11} + S_{21} + S_{31} \; = 665,000 + 35,000 + 41,000 = 741,000$$
$$S_2 = S_{12} + S_{22} + S_{32} = 19,000 + 910,000 + 410,000 = 1,339,000$$
$$S_3 = S_{13} + S_{23} + S_{33} = 1,216,000 + 2,555,000 + 3,649,000 = 7,420,000$$

(iii) Double-constrained gravity model for trip distribution

The final example in this chapter is the use of a gravity model to describe the *interaction* of activities rather than the *location* of activities. The model as used in this example describes the distribution of work trips, given the location of both workers (in zones of residence) and jobs (in employment zones). Remember that in the single-constrained model it was explained that the *location* of activities (the destination of expenditure or trips) was not constrained within the model. In traffic-distribution models, however, both the total origins and total destinations of trips will be known, and the model is used to describe how many trips there are between pairs of zones. This means that the model is not free to decide on the location of trip ends—both origins and destinations are constrained. The single-constrained gravity model is not therefore adequate as it stands for trip distribution studies. One way of solving the problem is to introduce another term into the model. With this additional term in, the model is known as the double-constrained gravity model, and the formula is:

$$T_{ij} = A_i B_j O_i D_j d_{ij}^{-b}$$

where T_{ij} = trips between zones i and j,

O_i = total number of trips originating in zone i,

D_j = total number of trips with destinations in j,

$A_i = (\sum_i B_j D_j d_{ij}^{-b})^{-1}$,

$B_j = (\sum_j A_i O_i d_{ij}^{-b})^{-1}$.

The additional term B_j will ensure that the two constraints

$$\sum_j T_{ij} = O_i$$

and

$$\sum_i T_{ij} = D_j$$

are satisfied; in other words both the known origins (O_i) and destinations (D_j) can be correctly obtained from the interaction data. The flowchart for the double-constrained model is shown in Fig. 5.3.

Notice that the expression for A_i includes the term B_j, while that for B_j includes A_i. This means that they must be calculated by iteration: this means setting the value of A_i at one and calculating the value of B_j. This

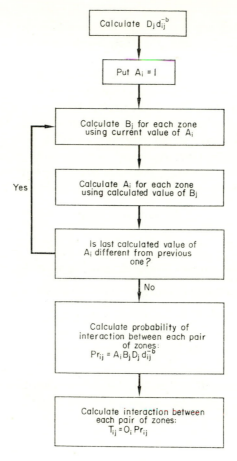

Fig. 5.3. Flowchart for double-constrained gravity model.

calculated value of B_j is then used to calculate a new value A_i, which will be different from the initial value. The new value of A_i is substituted into the equation for B_j, and a new value for B_j obtained. This is then substituted into the equation for A_i, and a new value for A_i calculated. This process is continued until there is no difference between the previous values of A_i and B_j and the newly calculated ones.

Using the data shown in Table 5.13, the first step (as before) is to calculate

$$D_j d_{ij}^{-b} \text{ (Table 5.14)}$$

for each pair of zones.

TABLE 5.13

Zone	Resident workers (O_i)	Employment (D_j)
1	8800	4000
2	16,210	8000
3	18,990	32,000
Total	44,000	44,000

The next step is to calculate the A_i's and the B_j's by iteration. The calculation can be tedious; this example required five iterations to arrive at the values of A_i and B_j for each of three zones, that is, a total of 30

TABLE 5.14. CALCULATION OF $D_j d_{ij}^{-2}$

i \ j	j = 1	j = 2	j = 3
i = 1	$\dfrac{4000}{2^2} = 1000$	$\dfrac{8000}{8^2} = 125$	$\dfrac{32,000}{6^2} = 888 \cdot 89$
i = 2	$\dfrac{4000}{8^2} = 62 \cdot 5$	$\dfrac{8000}{3^2} = 888 \cdot 89$	$\dfrac{32,000}{4^2} = 2000$
i = 3	$\dfrac{4000}{6^2} = 111 \cdot 11$	$\dfrac{8000}{4^2} = 500$	$\dfrac{32,000}{3^2} = 3555 \cdot 56$

calculations. In fact the values for this example were calculated by using a computer program; the final results were:

$$A_1 = 1\cdot879$$
$$A_2 = 1\cdot070$$
$$A_3 = 0\cdot762$$
$$B_1 = 0\cdot00021$$
$$B_2 = 0\cdot00032$$
$$B_3 = 0\cdot00032$$

As before, we can now calculate the probability of interaction between the zones. This time, however, the expression to be evaluated is:

$$Pr_{ij} = A_i B_j D_j d_{ij}^{-2}.$$

$$Pr_{11} = A_1 B_1 (D_1 d_{11}^{-2}) = 1\cdot879 \times 0\cdot00021 \times 1000 \qquad = 0\cdot39$$
$$Pr_{12} = A_1 B_2 (D_2 d_{12}^{-2}) = 1\cdot879 \times 0\cdot00032 \times 125 \qquad = 0\cdot08$$
$$Pr_{13} = A_1 B_3 (D_3 d_{13}^{-2}) = 1\cdot879 \times 0\cdot00032 \times 888\cdot89 \qquad = 0\cdot53$$
$$Pr_{21} = A_2 B_1 (D_1 d_{21}^{-2}) = 1\cdot070 \times 0\cdot00021 \times 62\cdot5 \qquad = 0\cdot01$$
$$Pr_{22} = A_2 B_2 (D_2 d_{22}^{-2}) = 1\cdot070 \times 0\cdot00032 \times 888\cdot89 \qquad = 0\cdot30$$
$$Pr_{23} = A_2 B_3 (D_3 d_{23}^{-2}) = 1\cdot070 \times 0\cdot00032 \times 2000 \qquad = 0\cdot69$$
$$Pr_{31} = A_3 B_1 (D_1 d_{31}^{-2}) = 0\cdot762 \times 0\cdot00021 \times 111\cdot11 \qquad = 0\cdot02$$
$$Pr_{32} = A_3 B_2 (D_2 d_{32}^{-2}) = 0\cdot762 \times 0\cdot00032 \times 500 \qquad = 0\cdot12$$
$$Pr_{33} = A_3 B_3 (D_3 d_{33}^{-2}) = 0\cdot762 \times 0\cdot00032 \times 3555\cdot56 = 0\cdot86$$

We can now calculate the actual trips between zones:

$$T_{ij} = O_i Pr_{ij}.$$

$$T_{11} = O_1 Pr_{11} = 8800 \times 0\cdot39 = 3432$$
$$T_{12} = O_1 Pr_{12} = 8800 \times 0\cdot08 = 704$$
$$T_{13} = O_1 Pr_{13} = 8800 \times 0\cdot53 = 4664$$
$$T_{21} = O_2 Pr_{21} = 16210 \times 0\cdot01 = 162$$
$$T_{22} = O_2 Pr_{22} = 16210 \times 0\cdot3 = 4863$$
$$T_{23} = O_2 Pr_{23} = 16210 \times 0\cdot69 = 11185$$
$$T_{31} = O_3 Pr_{31} = 18990 \times 0\cdot02 = 380$$
$$T_{32} = O_3 Pr_{32} = 18990 \times 0\cdot12 = 2279$$
$$T_{33} = O_3 Pr_{33} = 18990 \times 0\cdot86 = 16331$$

Once again the results can be summarised in matrix form:

TABLE 5.15. $T_{ij} = O_i Pr_{ij}$

i \ j	$j = 1$	$j = 2$	$j = 3$	Total
$i = 1$	3432	704	4664	8800
$i = 2$	162	4863	11,185	16,210
$i = 3$	380	2279	16,331	18,990
Total	3974	7846	32,180	44,000

Notice that the destinations in each zone j are quite close to the known (input) values of employment:

TABLE 5.16. ACTUAL AND PREDICTED TRIP
DESTINATIONS

Zone	Actual D_j	Predicted D_j
1	4000	3974
2	8000	7846
3	32,000	32,180

The slight differences can be accounted for by rounding errors due to the manual calculation, and to the fact that the iterations on the A_j's and B_j's were not allowed to continue until the values converged even more.

The reader who would like to see reports of the operational use of gravity models can usefully consult the works by McLoughlin (1966) and Freeman, Fox, Wilbur Smith and Assoc. (1966) listed at the end of the chapter. A comprehensive review of the theory and practice of the use of gravity models is to be found in the work edited by Styles (1968).

D

REFERENCES

BATTY, M. (1970) An activity allocation model for the Notts/Derby sub-region. *Regional Studies*, vol. 4, no. 3.

BROADBENT, T. A. (1969) *Zone size and spatial interaction*. Centre for Environmental Studies, Working Note 106.

CARROLL, J. D. and BEVIS, H. W. (1957) Predicting local travel in urban regions. *Papers and Proceedings of Regional Science Association*, vol. 3.

CORDEY HAYES (1968) *Retail Location Models*. Centre for Environmental Studies, Working Paper 16.

CRIPPS, E. L. (1968) *Limitations of the Gravity Concept*, in Styles (1968).

CRIPPS, E. L. and CARTER, E. (1971) *The Empirical Development of a Disaggregated Residential Location Model: Some Preliminary Results*. Urban Systems Research Unit, University of Reading, Working Paper 9.

FREEMAN, FOX, WILBUR SMITH and ASSOC. (1966): *London Traffic Survey*, vol. II. Greater London Council.

HANSEN, W. G. (1959) How accessibility shapes land use. *Journal of the American Institute of Planners*, May.

ISARD, W. (1960) *Methods of Regional Analysis*. M.I.T. Press.

LAKSHMANAN, T. R. and HANSEN, W. G. (1965) A retail market potential model. *Journal of American Institute of Planners*, May.

LEWIS, J. P. (1970) The invasion of planning. *Journal of the Town Planning Institute*, May.

MCLOUGHLIN, J. B. *et al.* (1966) *Regional Shopping Centres in North West England*, Part II. University of Manchester.

SCHNEIDER, M. (1959) Gravity models and trip distribution theory. *Papers and Proceedings of the Regional Science Association*, vol. 5.

STYLES, B. J. (Ed.) (1968) *Gravity Models in Town Planning*. Lanchester Polytechnic.

TANNER, J. C. (1961) *Some Factors affecting the Amount of Travel*. Road Research Laboratory Paper No. 58.

WILSON, A. G. (1969a) The use of entropy maximising methods in the theory of trip distribution. *Journal of Transport Economics and Policy*, vol. 3, no. 1.

WILSON, A. G. (1969b) *Disaggregating Elementary Residential Models*. Centre for Environmental Studies, Working Paper 37.

WILSON, A. G. (1969c) *Entropy in Urban and Regional Modelling*. Centre for Environmental Studies, Working Paper 26.

CHAPTER 6

The Lowry Model

INTRODUCTION

The Lowry model has probably generated more interest (and literature!) than any other single urban model. It has been quite widely used and extensively written about. It represents a significant step forward in our modelling ability, and therefore deserves careful attention from those who would understand the contribution that modelling is making and can make to the work of the planner.

The organisation of the chapter is as follows:

   (i) Partial and general models.
  (ii) The general structure of the Lowry model.
 (iii) The economic base mechanism.
 (iv) The location of activities.
  (v) The integration of the economic base and allocation mechanisms.
 (vi) Problems and limitations.
(vii) Examples of use.

PARTIAL AND GENERAL MODELS

In the last few chapters we have examined some of the models which have been used for forecasting the distribution of the major activities in the urban system, and the interaction between activities. All of the models which have been described are in fact partial sub-system models—they deal only with individual parts of the urban system, and must be linked heuristically by the user if he is interested in the interaction between sub-systems (a heuristic is an intuitive short-cut procedure used by human beings faced with complex situations, and based on appropriate experience). We know, however, that it is this interaction in which we are particularly interested, as the location patterns of the major urban activities are closely interconnected. Because of this, the independent sub-system models which have been developed to date must be regarded as representing a transient stage in our ability to model the urban system. The ultimate objective must be to develop a model which explicitly recognises and includes the interactions between sub-systems. However, we are at the present time a long way from having a general model of the urban system (i.e. a model which incorporates all the major elements of the urban system), and it is probable that we will never be able to develop a completely general urban model, because of our inability to fully describe and understand all the interactions in the complex economic and social systems which are present in an urban area. Batty (1971a) suggests that given our present state of know-ledge, any model which tries to represent two or more sub-systems may be regarded as a "general" model. There have been two notable attempts to develop models which represent several aspects of the urban system: the now famous Lowry model (Lowry, 1964) and the more recent application by Jay Forrester of dynamic simulation techniques to the modelling of urban systems (Forrester, 1969). Forrester's system dynamics methodology is still at a very early stage of development: we will therefore concentrate in this chapter on the Lowry model as an example of the move towards the development of a general urban systems model.

THE GENERAL STRUCTURE OF THE LOWRY MODEL

We made the distinction at an early stage between the use of models for forecasting the levels of urban activities and for locating a previously determined level of activity. The Lowry model introduced two major innovations into the urban modelling field: first, it incorporated within its structure both a forecasting and an allocation procedure; second it related three elements of the urban system together within one model framework. The model takes what Lowry assumed to be the three major components of metropolitan areas—population, employment, and the means of com-munication between them (i.e. the transport network, as represented by journey times)—and describes the interactions between them, and the way that these interactions determine urban change.

The *levels* of activities in the Lowry model are determined by the economic base method. The *location* of activities was determined in the original Lowry formulation by sub-models based on potential models, but more recent versions (including all of the applications in this country) have used gravity models as the basis of the allocation rules.

THE ECONOMIC BASE MECHANISM

Economic base theory has been extensively used by planners in the United States as the basis of economic forecasting methods, and is commanding growing interest among British planners. Economic base theory divides the activity of an area into two sectors. The "export" or "basic" sector produces goods which are mainly consumed outside the area, and whose growth is therefore basically related to national economic growth; the growth of "service" or "locally dependent" industries on the other hand is dependent on the growth in population of the local area—the population which provides the labour force for the basic industries will create a demand for services such as retailing, banking, transport, etc.

The major force driving changes in the structure of an urban region is therefore (according to economic base theory) change in employment in the region's "basic" industries, for this affects population and employment levels directly (i.e. those people employed in basic industry) and indirectly (because it is the population dependent on "basic" industry who generate the demand for service employment).

The distinction between population dependent on "basic" employment and "service" employment is central to the way in which both the forecasting and the locational parts of the recent versions of the Lowry model operate, and it will be useful to see how the propositions of the economic base method are expressed in equation form.

The first proposition that we examined suggested that the economic activity of an area can be divided into two basic categories, "basic" and "service". If we measure economic activity in an urban area by the number of people employed we can say that total employment consists of (a) those people employed in basic industries and (b) those people employed in service industries. If we represent total employment by E, basic employment by B, and service employment by S, then we can say

$$E = B + S. \tag{1}$$

As planners we are also interested in the relationship between levels of economic activity and population levels. At any one time, a given number of total jobs, E, will support a certain number of people, P. If we represent the number of people supported by one job by the symbol α, then we know that

$$P = \alpha E. \tag{2}$$

α is obviously a rate or factor which reflects the proportion of the total population which is employed. It can therefore be thought of as a population multiplier, expressing the ratio of total population (P) to total employment (E) and can be found at any one time by dividing the total population P by total employment (E). In other words:

$$\alpha = P/E. \tag{3}$$

If we know the value of α then, for any given level of total employment, E, we can find the level of population that will be supported, by multiplying the number of jobs (E) by α. Thus if at one point in time there were 2000 jobs and 6000 people, α would be equal to 3 ($\alpha = P/E = 6000/2000$). If the number of future jobs was expected to be 4000, then using the economic base method, the future population would be estimated using equation (2) as follows:

$$P = \alpha E = 3 \times 4000 = 12{,}000.$$

However, we have already suggested that the important relationships on which the Lowry model is based are concerned with the distinction between population which is dependent on "basic" employment and that dependent upon "service" employment. What we are interested in therefore is an equation which expresses population in terms of basic and service employment, rather than total employment.

This is quite easy to obtain. We have already seen (equation (2)) that population is a function of total employment:

$$P = \alpha E.$$

But we have also seen, in equation (1), that total employment is equal to basic employment plus service employment:

$$E = B + S.$$

We can therefore substitute $(B + S)$ for E in equation (2), which becomes:

$$P = \alpha(B + S). \tag{4}$$

In other words, we are simply saying that population is some function (α) of basic plus service employment. If we rewrite equation (4), by multiplying out the expression on the right-hand side, we then have

$$P = \alpha B + \alpha S \tag{5}$$

in which αB is the population dependent on basic employment and αS is the population dependent on service employment.

The second proposition of economic base theory which is important for the operation of the Lowry model is that the level of service employment is determined by the level of population. Therefore, just as we said that population is some function of total employment, we can say that service employment is a function of total population. If we say that

$$S = \beta P \tag{6}$$

then β can be thought of as a population-serving ratio—a factor which expresses the amount of service employment which will be demanded or supported by a given population. It is the ratio of service employment to total population, and the value at β at any one time can be found by dividing the number of service jobs by the total population. We can therefore define β as follows:

$$\beta = S/P. \tag{7}$$

We can now see the way in which the economic base method is used to forecast population and employment. Given values for α and β, and a forecast of the number of basic jobs, the population dependent on basic employment is found by multiplying the number of basic jobs by the population multiplier. In other words, if B is the number of basic jobs, and $P(1)$ is the population dependent on basic employment, then:

$$P(1) = \alpha B. \tag{8}$$

We know that this population will generate a demand for, and is capable of supporting, a number of jobs in service industry, and that this number is reflected in the value of the population serving ratio β. We can therefore find the number of service jobs demanded by the basic population $P(1)$ as follows:

$$D(1) = \beta P(1). \tag{9}$$

However, we also know that these service workers will themselves have dependent population, and if we call this dependent population $P(2)$, we can say:

$$P(2) = \alpha D(1).$$

But this additional population will itself generate a demand for service employment $D(2)$, so that:

$$D(2) = \beta P(2).$$

Similarly the latest increment of service employment $D(2)$ will have its own dependent population $(P(3))$ and this in turn will generate another increment of service employment, and so on. In fact each increment of service employment and service dependent population becomes smaller, until they become insignificant. The sum of the increments of service employment $(D(1)+D(2) = D(3)+...+D(N))$ represents the total forecast service employment, and the sum of the increments of population is the total service dependent population. When the increments have become insignificant, the totals are said to have converged.

THE LOCATION OF ACTIVITIES

The planner's concern is not only with changes in the levels of employment and population, but also with the possible alternative locations of these activities within the region. Given the location of basic employment, or even assuming changes in industrial location, the problem may be seen as one of discovering where the population would live in relation to the employment opportunities provided. Alternatively, the problem may be expressed as one of discovering which policies in terms of the location of basic industry can achieve the desired pattern of development.

In the original Lowry model, population was distributed using a potential model (similar to the Hansen residential model), in which the amount of population allocated to any one zone was determined by the sum of the inter-zonal potentials for that zone, i.e.

$$P_j = G \sum_{i=1}^{n} \frac{E_i}{d_{ij}} \qquad (10)$$

where P_j is the amount of population allocated to j,

     E_i is basic employment in i,

     d_{ij} is a trip index reflecting the impedance or deterrence factor between i and j,

     G is a scaling factor to ensure that $\sum_j P_j$ is equal to the total population growth forecast (P).

The most widely used versions of the Lowry model, however, are based on the adaptations suggested by Garin (Garin, 1966) who used measures of interaction based on the gravity model. In the residential activity system, for example, population is distributed from workplaces by calculating the probability of interaction between any two zones, and multiplying the probability of interaction by the amount of activity to be allocated: this is the basis of the single-constrained gravity model as developed in Chapter 5:

$$T_{ij} = E_i A_i P_j d_{ij}^{-1} \qquad (11)$$

where E_i is the total amount of activity to be allocated from zone j

     (i.e. people employed in zone i);

     T_{ij} is the amount of activity allocated from zone i to zone j.

The expression:

$$A_i P_j d_{ij}^{-1} \quad \text{(where } A_i = (\sum_{j=1}^{n} P_j d_{ij}^{-1})^{-1})$$

is the probability of interaction between zones i and j, with P_j being a measure of the attraction of zone (see Chapter 5). The total number of workers living in any one zone j is therefore

$$\sum_{i=1}^{n} T_{ij}.$$

The total amount of population living in any zone then becomes

$$P_j = \alpha \sum_{i=1}^{n} T_{ij}$$

or, in other words, the number of workers living in zone j multiplied by the population multiplier (α).

In all applications to date, the measure of the attraction of any zone which has been incorporated is existing population. If we represent existing population in zone j by P_j and adopt the symbolic conventions of Chapter 5 we can write the residential location component of the Garin–Lowry model as

$$T_{ij} = A_i E_i P_j d_{ij}^{-b} \tag{12}$$

where

$$A_i = (\sum_j P_j d_{ij}^{-b})^{-1}. \tag{13}$$

THE INTEGRATION OF THE ECONOMIC BASE AND ALLOCATION MECHANISMS

In fact we have suggested that the model is concerned not only with total workers and total population, but with "basic" and "service" employees, and therefore with the population dependent on basic jobs and population dependent on service jobs. Following the amendments suggested by Garin most applications of the model take this distinction into account by integrating the economic base and the allocation procedure. This is achieved by operating the residential location component of the model (the gravity model) first for only basic employees. The location of basic employment is an input to the model; the first operation within the model is then to allocate these basic employees to zones using the gravity model as described above. Now, however, E_i represents only *basic* workers in zone i, and T_{ij} is the number of basic employees who work in zone i and live in zone j. We can now find the basic population living in zone j by multiplying the total number of basic workers living in j ($\Sigma_i \, T_{ij}$) by the population multiplier, α. If we represent the basic population in j by $P_j(1)$ then:

$$P_j(1) = \alpha \sum_i T_{ij}. \tag{14}$$

But we know that the basic population in each zone will generate a demand for services which will result in service employment, and that the amount of service employment generated per head of population is represented by the population serving ratio. The first increment of service employment, $D_j(1)$, is found by applying the population serving ratio β to the basic population resident in each zone:

$$D_j(1) = \beta P_j(1). \tag{15}$$

This is the demand for service employment which is generated by the people living in zone j. The next step is to allocate this employment to service employment centres. This is done using the same form of the single-constrained gravity model as was used for residential location:

$$S_{ji}(1) = B_j D_j(1) S_i d_{ji}^{-a} \tag{16}$$

where $\qquad B_j = (\sum_i S_i d_{ji}^{-a})^{-1}.$

Once again the measure of attraction of each zone is taken to be the existing level of activity (in this case service employment in zone i, S_i) in the zone. $S_{ji}(1)$ then represents the number of service employees demanded by population resident in zone j who work in zone i. The first increment of service employment $S_i(1)$ is therefore found by summing $S_{ji}(1)$ over j:

$$S_i(1) = \sum_j S_{ji}. \tag{17}$$

Note that this is the amount of service employment in one zone (i). The total amount of service employment in all zones is obtained by summing the service employment of each zone, i.e.

$$S(1) = \sum_i \sum_j S_{ji}. \tag{18}$$

We next have to find the increment of population dependent on $S_i(1)$. This is done by substituting $S_i(1)$ for $E_i(1)$ in equation (12); this enables the location of service workers in zones of residence to be calculated. Equation (15) then calculates service-dependent population by using the population multiplier, and the whole sequence of calculations is repeated until the increments become insignificant and the totals converge. The general structure and sequence of calculations of the model are illustrated in Fig. 6.1 which provides the basis for the worked example at the end of the chapter.

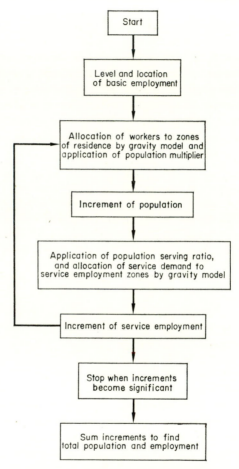

FIG. 6.1. Flowchart of Lowry model.

PROBLEMS AND LIMITATIONS OF THE
LOWRY MODEL

The Lowry model is relatively simple and easy to use, and this alone makes it an attractive proposition for the operational planner. It has now been used in several planning studies in this country, and has received considerable attention from practising planners and academics. Nevertheless, there are still problems related to the structure and operation of the model which limit its usefulness and validity as a planning tool. The references cited in the next section discuss in detail the theoretical and practical limitations of the Lowry model. The following points constitute some of the major and more obvious of these:

(i) The model is essentially a static one; it describes the urban system at only one point in time.

(ii) It is an equilibrium model: it assumes that all the activities represented in the model are in equilibrium throughout the whole study area. In fact there is always a dynamic, changing element in the urban system, but the Lowry model is not capable of representing it. Its static equilibrium nature makes it impossible to study directly the development of effects through time of different policies. The equilibrium nature of the model means that the effect of the existing stock on the location of activities is ignored: by allocating activities to an equilibrium position, it is assumed that all activities are free to move to the equilibrium location. In fact the location of a large amount of activity is heavily constrained by the existing stock of development. This means that changes in the system are usually of a marginal kind, but the effects of such marginal changes cannot be isolated in a "total stock" model which re-allocates the total amount of activity at one go.

(iii) Cordey Hayes *et al.* (1970) emphasise that it deals only with simplified relationships between highly aggregated variables. The whole of industry and commerce for example is represented by basic and service employment—there is no identification of different types of basic or service activities. Similarly the complexities of the housing market are modelled by consideration only

of the distance or cost between home and work and the attractiveness of a zone as a place of residence.

(iv) Both the residential and service employment sub-models are
essentially demand models, and implicitly assume that supply
meets demand, but do not consider the processes involved in this.
In reality the location of activities is likely to be very sensitive to
the supply side of the market, and the provision of stocks of
accommodation is related to many factors in addition to demand.

(v) Because the allocation component of the Lowry model is based on
the use of gravity models it is subject to the same criticisms made
of the gravity model (Chapter 5). There is no attempt within the
model to explain the complex factors which determine locational
behaviour. The allocation of activities is based on inferred analogy
rather than on an examination of the chain of cause and effect.
Largely as a result of this, it has been necessary to introduce constraints into the model to ensure that its performance is brought
into line with the real-world data. Batty (1970b) discusses in
detail some of the issues raised by the need to incorporate constraints into the original Lowry framework.

(vi) Related to the last point is the problem of measuring the relative
attraction of zones for the location of residential activities. The
"intrinsic" attractive power of a zone (i.e. "those attributes of an
area which make it attractive for residential development, but
which are unrelated to its proximity to workplaces" (Cordey
Hayes *et al.*, 1970)) is an essential component of the allocation
mechanism, but has not received very much attention, nor has a
satisfactory solution yet been found. One of the reasons why Batty
found that the model overpredicted population in some zones of
the Notts/Derby study was undoubtedly that the use of existing
population as a measure of attraction is unrealistic, and causes the
model to allocate population into areas which have already exceeded
their capacity to absorb population.

(vii) Because the forecasting, or derivation side of the model, is based
very strongly on an economic base mechanism the model has all
the weaknesses associated with economic base theory. As a result
of the particular way in which the economic base mechanism is
integrated into the allocation framework, and the way in which the

model is used, there may be a particular constraint on the range of possible policy-tests. Cordey Hayes *et al.* (1970) describe the problem as follows: "The growth of the basic sector of employment is assumed to be generated by factors outside the areal system being considered. If this assumption were valid, the absence of any feedback from internal growth to the amount of basic employment would be correct. However, as Tiebout (Tiebout, 1956) points out, growth may be initiated within the system itself by factors such as housing investment, business investment and local government expenditure, with a consequent feedback effect on the amount of so-called basic industry. Moreover, some of these factors which it is thought might influence the level of 'basic' industrial employment are under the control, or at least the partial control, of the planner. For example, it is an accepted feature of regional policy to attract basic industry by improving internal public services. The iteration sequence of the model as it stands makes it impossible to evaluate alternative plans for which such an increase in basic employment is an objective."

(viii) The model can be difficult to calibrate. The problems of calibrating gravity models have already been mentioned (Chapter 5) and will not be repeated here. The problems of calibration may however be increased in the Lowry model by the need to impose constraints on residential location. Batty (1970a, 1970b) discusses the procedures and problems of calibration much more fully than was done in Chapter 5.

Suggestions have been made for overcoming some of these deficiencies. Disaggregation of the critical variables—population and employment—can lead to a significant improvement in the theoretical basis of the model, and in its performance (Cripps and Batty, 1969; Wilson, 1970). There have also been attempts to overcome the static equilibrium nature of the model and to try to incorporate a dynamic element (Consad, 1964; Batty, 1971b). A great deal of work has also been done by the staff of the Centre for Environmental Studies in improving the theoretical base and the operational structure of the model (Cordey Hayes *et al.*, 1971).

It seems reasonable to agree with Batty's conclusion that "At present the model provides a reasonably good simulation device, and it can be extremely useful if used with care. It is manageable in terms of both technique and cost, and if it is integrated with objective techniques for design, and evaluation of the system, the planner can have a high confidence in the model's prediction" (Batty, 1970b).

The model obviously has limitations and deficiencies, but until a model is developed which has a better theoretical base and practical performance, the Lowry model is likely to remain one of the most widely used urban development models.

EXAMPLES OF USE

Because the Lowry model is more complex than the other models we have been considering, the amount of calculation involved is larger. However, the basic structure is really quite straightforward, as the flow-chart of Fig. 6.1 shows.

We will once again use our three-zone area as an example: all the necessary data are shown in Table 6.1 for convenience.

TABLE 6.1

Zone	Basic employment	Service employment	Total employment	Total population
1	2800	1200	4000	19,000
2	4000	4000	8000	35,000
3	12,000	20,000	32,000	41,000
Total	18,800	25,200	44,000	95,000

Time/distance matrix:

From \ To	1	2	3
1	2	8	6
2	8	3	4
3	6	4	3

We will assume that the two exponents *a* and *b* have a value of 2 from calibration.

What we are going to do is to use the Lowry model to predict the location of population and service employment, given the location of basic employment. Because we know what the actual locations are, we will be able to check the results of the model, but the actual data on population and service employment are not used during the operation of the model (except, of course, to calculate the ratios α and β and the attraction of zones. If the model were used for projection, α and β would be calculated from data for the base year).

The first step is to calculate the population multiplier and the population serving ratio from the known data:

$$\alpha = P/E = 95,000/44,000 = 2 \cdot 195,$$
$$\beta = S/P = 25,200/95,000 = 0 \cdot 265.$$

Next we need to allocate the basic employees, E_i, to zones of residence. This we do by using the single-constrained gravity model:

$$T_{ij} = E_i A_i P_j d_{ij}^{-2}$$

where

$$A_i = (\sum_j P_j d_{ij}^{-2})^{-1},$$

so that first we need to calculate the probability of interaction (as we did in the gravity model examples in Chapter 5), represented by the term

$$(Pr_{ij})^P = A_i P_i d_{ij}^{-2}.$$

To do this we must first calculate $(P_j d_{ij}^{-2})$ for each pair of zones:

TABLE 6.2. CALCULATION OF $P_i d_{ij}^{-2}$

i \ j	$j = 1$	$j = 2$	$j = 3$	$\sum_j P_j d_{ij}^{-2}$
$i = 1$	$\dfrac{19,000}{2^2} = 4750$	$\dfrac{35,000}{8^2} = 546 \cdot 88$	$\dfrac{41,000}{6^2} = 1138 \cdot 89$	$6435 \cdot 77$
$i = 2$	$\dfrac{19,000}{8^2} = 296 \cdot 88$	$\dfrac{35,000}{3^2} = 3888 \cdot 89$	$\dfrac{41,000}{4^2} = 2562 \cdot 5$	$6748 \cdot 27$
$i = 3$	$\dfrac{19,000}{6^2} = 527 \cdot 78$	$\dfrac{35,000}{4^2} = 2187 \cdot 5$	$\dfrac{41,000}{3^2} = 4555 \cdot 56$	$7270 \cdot 84$

We can now calculate the probability of interactions:

TABLE 6.3. CALCULATION OF $(Pr_{ij})^P = A_i P_j d_{ij}^{-2}$

i $\diagdown$ j	$j = 1$	$j = 2$	$j = 3$
$i = 1$	$\dfrac{4750}{6435 \cdot 77} = 0 \cdot 738$	$\dfrac{546 \cdot 88}{6435 \cdot 77} = 0 \cdot 085$	$\dfrac{1138 \cdot 89}{6435 \cdot 77} = 0 \cdot 177$
$i = 2$	$\dfrac{296 \cdot 88}{6748 \cdot 27} = 0 \cdot 044$	$\dfrac{3888 \cdot 89}{6748 \cdot 27} = 0 \cdot 576$	$\dfrac{2562 \cdot 5}{6748 \cdot 27} = 0 \cdot 380$
$i = 3$	$\dfrac{527 \cdot 78}{7270 \cdot 84} = 0 \cdot 073$	$\dfrac{2187 \cdot 5}{7270 \cdot 84} = 0 \cdot 301$	$\dfrac{4555 \cdot 56}{7270 \cdot 84} = 0 \cdot 626$

The allocation of basic employees to zones is straightforwardly calculated:

TABLE 6.4. CALCULATION OF $T_{ij}(1) = E_i (Pr_{ij})^P$

i $\diagdown$ j	$j = 1$	$j = 2$	$j = 3$
$i = 1$	$2800 \times 0 \cdot 738$ $= 2066$	$2800 \times 0 \cdot 085$ $= 238$	$2800 \times 0 \cdot 177$ $= 496$
$i = 2$	$4000 \times 0 \cdot 044$ $= 176$	$4000 \times 0 \cdot 576$ $= 2304$	$4000 \times 0 \cdot 380$ $= 1520$
$i = 3$	$12{,}000 \times 0 \cdot 073$ $= 876$	$12{,}000 \times 0 \cdot 301$ $= 3612$	$12{,}000 \times 0 \cdot 626$ $= 7512$
$\sum\limits_{i} T_{ij}(1)$	3118	6154	9528

Each entry in the table refers to the number of people employed in basic industry in zone i who live in zone j. The total workers living in any one zone therefore is found by adding the columns:

Total (basic) resident workers in each zone $j = \sum\limits_{i} T_{ij}(1)$.

In order to find the total "basic population" in each zone, we need to multiply the number of resident workers by the population multiplier (equation 14):

$$P_j(1) = \alpha . \sum_i T_{ij}(1)$$

$$= 2 \cdot 159 . \sum_i T_{ij}(1).$$

We can therefore calculate the "basic population" of each zone in turn:

$$P_1(1) = 2 \cdot 159 \sum_i T_{i1}(1) = 2 \cdot 159 \times 3118 = \quad 6732$$

$$P_2(1) = 2 \cdot 159 \sum_i T_{i2}(1) = 2 \cdot 159 \times 6154 = 13{,}286$$

$$P_3(1) = 2 \cdot 159 \sum_i T_{i3}(1) = 2 \cdot 159 \times 9528 = 20{,}571$$

We next need to find the service employment demanded by the population resident in each zone. We know from equation (15) that this is found by multiplying the resident population in each zone by the population serving ratio β:

$$D_j(1) = \beta P_j(1).$$

So that, for each zone in turn,

$$D_1(1) = 0 \cdot 265 \times P_1(1) = 0 \cdot 265 \times \quad 6732 = 1783$$
$$D_2(1) = 0 \cdot 265 \times P_2(1) = 0 \cdot 265 \times 13{,}286 = 3521$$
$$D_3(1) = 0 \cdot 265 \times P_3(1) = 0 \cdot 265 \times 20{,}571 = 5451$$

Now the service employment which has just been calculated must be located in service centres. Again we use a gravity model, this time locating jobs demanded by population in zones of residence (j) to zone of employment (i). Just as we calculated the probability of interaction for the population location model $(Pr_{ij})^P$, so now we must calculate the probability of interaction for the service employment location model. From equation (16)

$$S_{ji}(1) = B_j D_j(1) S_i d_{ji}^{-2}$$

where

$$B_j = (\sum_i S_i d_{ji}^{-2})^{-1}.$$

The probability of interaction, therefore, is:

$$(Pr_{ji})^S = B_j S_i d_{ji}^{-2}.$$

As before, we need to calculate $S_i d_{ji}^{-2}$ for each pair of zones, and then find the sum.

TABLE 6.5. CALCULATION OF $S_i d_i^{-2}$

i \ j	$j = 1$	$j = 2$	$j = 3$
$i = 1$	$\dfrac{1200}{2^2} = 300$	$\dfrac{1200}{8^2} = 18{\cdot}75$	$\dfrac{1200}{6^2} = 33{\cdot}33$
$i = 2$	$\dfrac{4000}{8^2} = 62{\cdot}5$	$\dfrac{4000}{3^2} = 444{\cdot}44$	$\dfrac{4000}{4^2} = 250$
$i = 3$	$\dfrac{20{,}000}{6^2} = 555{\cdot}56$	$\dfrac{20{,}000}{4^2} = 1250$	$\dfrac{20{,}000}{3^2} = 2222{\cdot}22$
$\sum\limits_i S_i d_{ji}^{-2}$	$918{\cdot}06$	$1713{\cdot}19$	$2505{\cdot}55$

We can now calculate $(Pr_{ji})^S$:

TABLE 6.6. $(Pr_{ji})^S = S_i d_{ji}^{-2} (\sum\limits_i S_i d_{ji}^{-2})^{-1}$

i \ j	$j = 1$	$j = 2$	$j = 3$
$i = 1$	$\dfrac{300}{918{\cdot}06} = 0{\cdot}33$	$\dfrac{18{\cdot}75}{1713{\cdot}19} = 0{\cdot}01$	$\dfrac{33{\cdot}33}{2505{\cdot}55} = 0{\cdot}01$
$i = 2$	$\dfrac{62{\cdot}5}{918{\cdot}06} = 0{\cdot}07$	$\dfrac{444{\cdot}44}{1713{\cdot}19} = 0{\cdot}26$	$\dfrac{250}{2505{\cdot}55} = 0{\cdot}10$
$i = 3$	$\dfrac{555{\cdot}56}{918{\cdot}06} = 0{\cdot}60$	$\dfrac{1250}{1713{\cdot}19} = 0{\cdot}73$	$\dfrac{2222{\cdot}22}{2505{\cdot}55} = 0{\cdot}89$

We are now in a position to allocate the service employment demanded by residents in each zone to zones of employment:

$$S_{ji} = D_j (1) (Pr_{ji})^S.$$
$$S_{11} = D_1 (1) (Pr_{11})^S = 1783 \times 0{\cdot}33 = 588$$
$$S_{12} = D_1 (1) (Pr_{12})^S = 1783 \times 0{\cdot}07 = 125$$

$$S_{13} = D_1 (1) (Pr_{13})^S = 1783 \times 0.60 = 1070$$
$$S_{21} = D_2 (1) (Pr_{21})^S = 3521 \times 0.01 = 35$$
$$S_{22} = D_2 (1) (Pr_{22})^S = 3521 \times 0.26 = 916$$
$$S_{23} = D_2 (1) (Pr_{23})^S = 3521 \times 0.73 = 2570$$
$$S_{31} = D_3 (1) (Pr_{31})^S = 5451 \times 0.01 = 55$$
$$S_{32} = D_3 (1) (Pr_{32})^S = 5451 \times 0.1 = 545$$
$$S_{33} = D_3 (1) (Pr_{33})^S = 5451 \times 0.89 = 4851$$

We have now calculated the location of service employment for each pair of zones. If we present the results in matrix form, as usual, we can find the total service employment in each zone:

TABLE 6.7. S_{ji}

i \ j	$j = 1$	$j = 2$	$j = 3$	$\sum_j S_{ji}$
$i = 1$	588	35	55	678
$i = 2$	125	916	545	1586
$i = 3$	1070	2570	4851	8491

We have now completed one iteration of the economic base mechanism—we have calculated one increment of population and service employment by working through equations (14) to (18).

We can summarise the results of this first iteration as follows:

TABLE 6.8

Zone	Basic employment	Increment of population	Increment of service employment
1	2800	6732	678
2	400	13,286	1586
3	12,000	20,571	8491

The model now operates the same sequence of calculations for as many iterations as are required to generate the necessary population and service employment. In fact 16 iterations are required to balance the population and employment totals for this example, but it is not necessary to work through all of these to demonstrate the principle. We will follow through one more iteration only, and then examine the results of all the iterations which were obtained by using a computer program. (The program used was originally written by M. Batty, ane has been modified by J. A. Yule at the University of Newcastle.)

The second iteration starts, not with basic employment as before, but with the increment of service employment which has just been calculated. The first step is to allocate the service employment to zones of residence; then calculate the population supported by the service employees; then calculate the additional demand for service employment which is generated by this new population; and finally allocate the additional service employment to employment zones.

The probabilities of interaction in both of the gravity models which are used for allocation remain unchanged from one iteration to another. Because they are not based on values which are produced by the economic base mechanism their values are determined by the known information which does not change between iterations (the reader can easily check this for himself). It is not therefore necessary to recalculate these probabilities.

First, then, we must locate the service employment in zones of residence: to do this, we substitute the value of $S_i(1)$ into equation (12) in place of

TABLE 6.9 $T_{ij}(2)$

i \\ j	$j = 1$	$j = 2$	$j = 3$
$i = 1$	$678 \times 0\cdot738$ $= 500$	$678 \times 0\cdot085$ $= 58$	$678 \times 0\cdot177$ $= 120$
$i = 2$	$1586 \times 0\cdot044$ $= 70$	$1586 \times 0\cdot576$ $= 914$	$1586 \times 0\cdot380$ $= 603$
$i = 3$	$8491 \times 0\cdot073$ $= 620$	$8491 \times 0\cdot301$ $= 2556$	$8491 \times 0\cdot626$ $= 5315$
$\sum_i T_{ij}(2)$	1190	3528	6038

E_i, so that:

$$T_{ij}(2) = S_i(1)(Pr_{ij})^P$$

where $(Pr_{ij})^P$ has already been calculated.

Next we calculate the resident population supported by the service workers:

$$P_j(2) = \alpha \sum_i T_{ij}(2)$$

so that

$$P_1(2) = 2\cdot159 \times 1190 = 2569$$

$$P_2(2) = 2\cdot159 \times 3528 = 7617$$

$$P_3(2) = 2\cdot159 \times 6038 = 13{,}036$$

This population again generates a demand for service employment:

$$D_j(2) = \beta P_j(2)$$

and

$$D_1(2) = 0\cdot265 \times 2569 = 681$$

$$D_2(2) = 0\cdot265 \times 7617 = 2019$$

$$D_3(2) = 0\cdot265 \times 13{,}036 = 3455$$

The additional service employment now needs to be located in employment zones. As before,

$$S_{ji}(2) = D_j(2)(Pr_{ji})^S.$$

TABLE 6.10. $S_{ji}(2)$

i \ j	$j = 1$	$j = 2$	$j = 3$	$\sum_j S_{ji}$
$i = 1$	$681 \times 0\cdot33$ $= 225$	$2019 \times 0\cdot01$ $= 20$	$3455 \times 0\cdot01$ $= 35$	280
$i = 2$	$681 \times 0\cdot07$ $= 48$	$2019 \times 0\cdot26$ $= 525$	$3455 \times 0\cdot10$ $= 346$	919
$i = 3$	$681 \times 0\cdot60$ $= 409$	$2019 \times 0\cdot73$ $= 1474$	$3455 \times 0\cdot89$ $= 3075$	4958

The results of the second iteration are shown in Table 6.11.

TABLE 6.11

Zone	Increment of population	Increment of service employment
1	2569	280
2	7617	919
3	13,036	4958

Notice that the increments of both population and employment are much smaller than those of the first iteration. They will in fact decrease with each further iteration. After the final iteration, the increments are added together to give the model's estimate of each of the activities (population and employment) by zone.

The increments from each iteration, together with the population and employment totals, are shown in Table 6.12.

TABLE 6.12. RESULTS OF 16 ITERATIONS OF THE LOWRY MODEL

Iteration no.	Service employment zone				Population zone			
	1	2	3	Total	1	2	3	Total
1	678	1586	8491	10,755	6732	13,286	20,571	40,589
2	280	919	4958	6157	2569	7617	13,036	23,222
3	155	528	2849	3532	1339	4408	7596	13,343
4	87	303	1633	2023	743	2536	4346	7625
5	50	174	935	1159	424	1454	2490	4368
6	28	99	536	663	242	833	1426	2501
7	16	57	307	380	139	477	817	1433
8	9	33	176	218	79	273	468	820
9	5	19	101	125	46	156	268	470
10	3	11	58	72	26	90	153	269
11	2	6	33	41	15	51	88	154
12	1	4	19	24	9	29	50	88
13	1	2	11	14	5	17	29	51
14	0	1	6	7	3	10	17	30
15	0	1	4	5	2	6	9	17
16	0	0	2	2	1	3	5	9
Total	1315	3743	20,119	25,177	12,374	31,246	51,369	94,989

We can now show the final output of the model (Tables 6.13, 6.14).

TABLE 6.13

Zone	Actual basic employment	Predicted service employment	Predicted total employment	Predicted total population
1	2800	1315	4115	12,374
2	4000	3743	7743	31,246
3	12,000	20,119	32,119	51,369
Total	18,800	25,177	43,977	94,989

If we compare the predicted figures of zonal employment and population with the actual figures, we can see how well the model has reproduced the known patterns of activities:

TABLE 6.14

Zone	Service employment		Total employment		Total population	
	Actual	Predicted	Actual	Predicted	Actual	Predicted
1	1200	1315	4000	4115	19,000	12,374
2	4000	3743	8000	7743	35,000	31,246
3	20,000	20,119	32,000	32,119	41,000	51,369
Total	25,200	25,177	44,000	43,977	95,000	94,989

The model appears to have been quite successful in predicting both the levels and the distribution of employment, but although the total population is accurate, the predicted distribution of population is not very good. However, as the data are completely hypothetical, the results have no meaning in themselves.

There have been several applications of the Lowry model in this country. These use a different technique to achieve convergence and do not depend upon repeated iterations of the kind which have been shown purely as a demonstration of the principle involved. The problems of operational use are well documented and the writer has found the reports of Batty (1969, 1970a, b), Cripps and Foot (1969a, 1969b), Thorburn *et al.* (1969) and Cordey Hayes *et al.* (1971) to be particularly useful. All of these in turn have extensive bibliographies.

REFERENCES

BATTY, M. (1969) The impact of a new town: an application of the Garin–Lowry model. *Journal of the Town Planning Institute*, vol. 55.

BATTY, M. (1970a) Some problems of calibrating the Lowry model. *Environment and Planning*, vol. 2.

BATTY, M. (1970b) An activity allocation model for Notts/Derby subregion. *Regional Studies*, vol. 4, no. 3.

BATTY, M. (1971a) *Introductory Model Building Problems for Urban and Regional Planning*. Urban Systems Research Unit, University of Reading.

BATTY, M. (1971b) Dynamic simulation of an urban system, in A. G. Wilson (Ed.), *Patterns and Processes in Urban Systems*, Pion, London.

CONSAD RESEARCH CORPORATION (1964) *A Time Oriented Metropolitan Model*. Pittsburgh Community Renewal Program, Technical Bulletin No. 6.

CORDEY HAYES, M. *et al.* (1970) *Towards Operational Urban Development Models*. Centre for Environmental Studies, Working Paper 60.

CORDEY HAYES, M. *et al.* (1971) *Project Report on an Operational Urban Development Model*. Centre for Environmental Studies, Working Paper 64.

CRIPPS, E. L. and BATTY, M. (1969) *Outline of Research in the Urban Systems Research Unit*. University of Reading.

CRIPPS, E. L. and FOOT, D. H. S. (1969a) The empirical development of an elementary residential location model. *Environment and Planning*, vol. 1.

CRIPPS, E. L. and FOOT, D. H. S. (1969b) A land use model for sub-regional planning. *Regional Studies*, vol. 3.

FORRESTER, J. (1969) *Urban Dynamics*, M.I.T. Press.

GARIN, R. A. (1966) A matrix formulation of the Lowry model for intra-metropolitan activity location. *Journal of the American Institute of Planners*, vol. 32.

ISARD, W. (1960) *Methods of Regional Analysis*. M.I.T. Press.

LOWRY, I. S. (1964) *A Model of Metropolis*. The Rand Corporation No. R.M. 4125 R.C.

PFOUTS, R. (1960) *The Techniques of Urban Economic Analysis*. Chandler Davis.

TIEBOUT, C. M. (1956) Exports and regional economic growth. *Journal of Political Economy*, April 1956.

THORBURN *et al.* (1969) *Proceedings of Seminar on Notts/Derby Planning Process*. Centre for Environmental Studies, Information Paper 11.

WILSON, A. G. (1970) *Disaggregating elementary residential location models*. Centre for Environmental Studies, Working Paper 37.

CHAPTER 7

Optimising Models

INTRODUCTION

It was suggested in Chapter 1 that mathematical models can be divided into three categories, the third of which was "planning" or "optimising" models. Mathematical optimising techniques are complex in detail, but the principles upon which they are based are fairly easy to understand. This chapter is concerned with the principle but not the detail of the operation of optimising models. The chapter is organised as follows:

(i) Optimising models as a planning tool.

(ii) Graphical solution of an optimisation problem.

(iii) Problems and limitations.

OPTIMISING MODELS AS A PLANNING TOOL

Planning models were described in Chapter 1 as "models which produce the plan which best satisfies the stated objectives, subject to the availability of resources and the constraints which are specified". Planning models are based on mathematical optimising techniques which have been developed to solve the general problem of the allocation of scarce resources.

There are two reasons why attention has been turned to the use of mathematical optimising techniques. First, the "traditional" evaluation process (consisting of the evaluation by various means of a number of alternative plans) has been felt to be unsatisfactory, largely because there

113

has often been a feeling that there might always be an alternative which may be "better", while there will always be limitations on the number of alternatives that can be tested. Secondly there seems to be a direct relationship between the essential objectives of planning and the problems for the solution of which mathematical programming techniques were developed (the allocation of limited resources among competing activities in an optimal manner), so that the possibility of using such techniques within the planning process appears worthy of investigation at least. A recent report of an application of optimising techniques (Ben-Shahar *et al.*, 1969) made the case for the use of optimising models in planning as follows:

> "Town planning is an operation under which for each unit of land its designated use and the intensity of this use for each future time period is determined. The goal of the town planner is to make a plan that maximises the value of a social welfare function subject to a number of constraints. Until recently, town planning was generally considered as primarily an architectural problem. Yet from the definition of its goal it follows that town planning is tightly connected with the social sciences. And moreover, the formulation of the goal as a maximisation process naturally calls for the utilisation of mathematical programming techniques."

The easiest of the mathematical optimisation techniques to use (and the one which has been most frequently used in planning applications—although it is still not a widespread tool) is *linear programming*. It is also the one that is most easily abused. This chapter is concerned with the principles of the linear programming technique. It will not deal with the more complex techniques of dynamic or integer programming which exist for the solution of problems which cannot be handled by linear programming methods. Nor will it deal with the mathematical methods for solving linear programming problems, as there are standard computer programs which handle the solution without the user knowing anything about the mathematical methods employed. However, the user of a linear programming "package" should be able to formulate his problem in the appropriate way, and he should understand what the program is doing, even if he does not understand how it is doing it. The objective of this chapter is to help the reader to understand what kind of problems are appropriate for a linear programming solution, and what such a solution means.

GRAPHICAL SOLUTION OF AN OPTIMISING PROBLEM

The easiest way to get some idea of the type of problem that can be tackled by linear programming methods is to consider a simplified example. Assume that there is an area of 50 acres of land which is to be developed by a Local Authority for residential use, and that two different types of houses—we will call them A and B—can be built. The density of type A houses is 10 units per acre; of type B houses 5 units per acre. Each type A house costs £2000, each type B costs £6000. The Local Authority's housing budget is £1,200,000. The rateable value of type A houses is £190 per unit, of type B £470 per unit. The problem is to control the mixture of house types in such a way as to provide the maximum rateable value for the Local Authority.

The components of the problem in linear programming terms are:

(i) the objective function which is to be optimised,

(ii) the constraints, which restrict the range of feasible solutions,

(iii) the variables, which are elements of the objective function.

The objective function in the example is the total additional rateable value. If A and B represent the number of type A and type B houses built, then the additional rateable value is $(190A + 470B)$. For instance if ten type A's ($A = 10$) and twenty type B's ($B = 20$) were built, the additional rateable value would be:

$$\text{Rateable value} = (£190 \times 10) + (£470 \times 20) = £11,300.$$

If one hundred of each type were built, the additional rateable value would be £66,000. An essential feature of linear programming is that the objective function should be of this linear form, consisting of a weighted sum of the variables (in this case A and B). The aim may be to maximise or minimise the objective function. In the example the aim is to maximise the additional rateable value, i.e. to find the maximum value of $(190A + 470B)$.

The constraints, or limitations on the use of resources, must also be linear (we will return to this question of linearity later). In the example there are two constraints: one on the maximum area of land to be developed (a land constraint) and one on the amount of finance available for housing construction (a budgetary constraint). The land constraint means that the number of houses constructed must not use more than the available supply of land. It provides that:

$$\tfrac{1}{10}A + \tfrac{1}{5}B \text{ must not exceed 50 acres.}$$

The budgetary constraint provides that the total cost of houses built must not exceed the available finance. In other words:

$$2000A + 6000B \text{ must not exceed } £1,200,000.$$

Alternatively these may be expressed as:

$$\tfrac{1}{10}A + \tfrac{1}{5}B \leq 50 \text{ acres,}$$

$$2000A + 6000B \leq £1,200,000.$$

The optimum policy might appear to be to build only type B houses. After all, they add £470 per unit to the authority's rateable value, against only £190 for each unit of type A. A total of 250 type B houses could be built on 50 acres, giving a total rateable value of £117,500 (250 × £470). However, the cost of this would be £1,500,000 (250 × £6000), which exceeds the budgetary constraint. The maximum number of type B houses which can be built without exceeding the available finance is 200 (£1,200,000 ÷ £6000). This would provide an additional rateable value of £94,000, but would leave 10 acres of land unused.

It is obvious from this preliminary consideration of the problem that the constraints are going to play an important part in the solution of the problem. As we are going to find the optimal solution by a simple graphical method, we will start by explaining the meaning of the constraints in graphical terms. The constraints are linear, therefore we would expect them to be described by a straight line. What we have to do is to find some way of translating the information about the constraints into a line on a graph. If we start with the land constraint, we know that

$$\tfrac{1}{10}A + \tfrac{1}{5}B \leq 50.$$

If for the moment we regard this as being equivalent to

$$\tfrac{1}{10}A + \tfrac{1}{5}B = 50$$

we can use this equation to obtain several values of A with their corresponding values of B. We can do this by rearranging the equation so that we can find the value of B in terms of A, as follows:

$$\tfrac{1}{10}A + \tfrac{1}{5}B = 50.$$

Subtract $(\tfrac{1}{10}A)$ from both sides:

$$\tfrac{1}{5}B = 50 - \tfrac{1}{10}A.$$

Multiply both sides by 5:

$$B = 250 - \tfrac{1}{2}A.$$

Using this equation, we can obtain the value of B for any given value of A. The table below shows a number of pairs of values for the two variables calculated from this equation for B.

A	B
0	250
100	200
200	150
300	100
400	50
500	0

This table represents combinations of numbers of type A and type B houses, each of which satisfies the land constraint, i.e. each combination shown in the table would use 50 acres of land. If these points were plotted on a graph, and joined by a line, the results would be as shown in Fig. 7.1. The line shown in Fig. 7.1 represents not only the six points which are tabulated and plotted on the graph. Any point on the line represents combinations of house types A and B which do not exceed the land constraint. However, the original constraint was expressed in terms of an inequality ($\tfrac{1}{10}A + \tfrac{1}{5}B \leq 50$), and not an equation. The inequality is represented graphically by any point on the line or in the shaded area of Fig. 7.1:

points on the line represent the "equal" part of the "less than or equal to" symbol, while any point in the shaded area represents a combination of house types which use less than 50 acres.

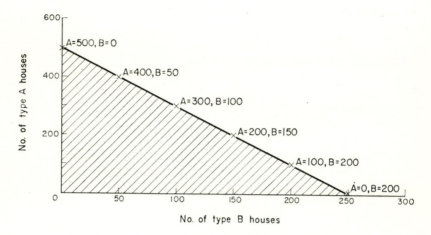

Fig. 7.1. Graphical representation of land constraint:
$\frac{1}{10}A + \frac{1}{3}B \leq 50$ acres.

We can carry out exactly the same procedure for the budgetary constraint. Again expressing the constraint initially as an equality, we know that

$$2000A + 6000B = 1,200,000.$$

Subtract $(2000A)$ from both sides:

$$6000B = 1,200,000 - 2000A.$$

Divide each side by 6000:

$$B = 200 - \tfrac{2}{6}A.$$

We can now use this equation to calculate a series of values for A and B, each pair of values representing a combination of house types, the total cost of which is equal to the finance available for house building.

A	*B*
0	200·0
100	166·7
200	133·4
300	100·0
400	66·7
500	33·4
600	0·0

We can now use the values in this table to show the budgetary constraint in graphical form, as in Fig. 7.2.

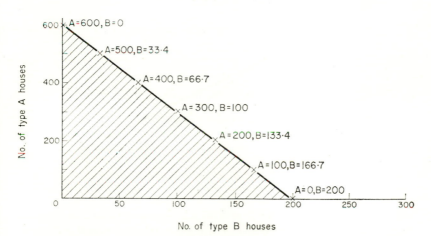

FIG. 7.2. Graphical representation of budgetary constraint:
$2000A + 6000B \leqq £1,200,000.$

As before, any point on the line represents a combination of house types, the construction cost of which is equal to the budgetary constraint, while any point in the shaded area represents a combination which has a construction cost less than the budgetary constraint.

In Fig. 7.3 both constraints are plotted on the same graph, but this time the shaded area is that part of the graph which lies below both constraint

E

lines. Any point within the triangle ABC violates the land constraint, i.e. any point in that area represents a combination of house types which would need more than the 50 acres of available land. Similarly any point within the triangle CDE exceeds the budgetary constraint. Any point beyond the line ACE would violate both constraints. The shaded area therefore represents combinations of policies which do not violate either of the constraints, i.e. these policies are feasible, in terms of the constraints, and this area is therefore known as the feasible area. Any point in the feasible area represents a combination of house types which does not use

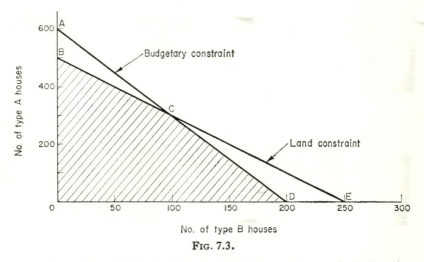

FIG. 7.3.

more than the available land, and which does not exceed the housing budget. In the remaining figures we will show only the feasible area on the graph, as this is really the only area in which we are interested. We are now in a position to see how the optimum policy may be selected. We know that any point on the graph represents a particular level of rateable value, because any combination of numbers of house types A and B can be converted to rateable value. The expression which enables us to do this is:

$$\text{Rateable value} = 190A + 470B.$$

The optimum policy is represented by the point in the feasible area which provides the greatest possible rateable value (or the largest possible value for the expression $190A + 470B$). The essence of a linear programming computation is the search for this point. A computer program determines this point by algebraic methods, but the principle can be demonstrated by simple graphical methods.

We know that the expression relating the number of house types to total rateable value is a linear one, similar in form to the expression of the constraints. We would expect therefore that the expression can be represented graphically by a straight line. If we start with an arbitrary figure of rateable value—say £40,000—we can work out which combinations of house types will provide this amount, and draw the line representing the relationship

$$190A + 470B = 40,000.$$

We do this by solving the equation ($190A + 470B = 40,000$) first for A, and then for B.

Solving for A:

$$190A + 470B = 40,000.$$

Subtract ($470B$) from both sides:

$$190A = 40,000 - 470B.$$

Divide each side by 190:

$$A = 210 - 2{\cdot}5B.$$

Solving for B:

$$190A + 470B = 40,000.$$

Subtract ($190A$) from both sides:

$$470B = 40,000 - 190A.$$

Divide each side by 470:

$$B = 85 - 0{\cdot}4A.$$

Therefore when $B = 0$, $A = 210$, and when $A = 0$, $B = 85$. As these two pairs of values represent the points at which the line described by the equation meets the A and B axes of the graph respectively, we can draw the line directly from these two points alone. This is shown in Fig. 7.4.

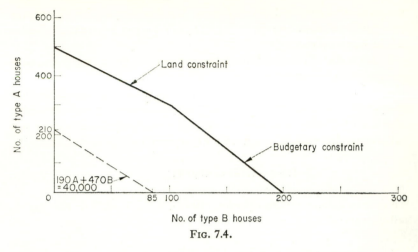

FIG. 7.4.

However, the line shown in Fig. 7.4 is only one of many which could be drawn from the relationship (Rateable value = $190A + 470B$). A series of lines could be drawn from this one relationship, each corresponding to a different level of rateable value. Figure 7.5, for example, shows three such lines, representing £40,000, £70,000, and £100,000 rateable value. Each of these lines was constructed in the same way as the one shown in Fig. 7.4.

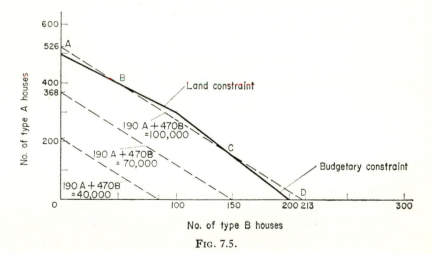

FIG. 7.5.

There are three particularly important features of Fig. 7.5. The first is that the three lines are parallel—they have the same slope. We would in fact expect this, because they are all derived from the same equation, and only the values of the variables are different. The second is that the farther we go from the origin, the greater the rateable value associated with the line. Again, we would expect this, because the greater the distance between the line and the origin the greater is the value of A and B. Remembering that A and B represent numbers of each house type built, it is obvious that as these numbers increase, so must the value of the expression (Rateable value $= 190A + 470B$). The third feature of Fig. 7.5 which is significant relates to the position of the line AD, representing a rateable value of £100,000. Notice that of the three lines on the graph, AD is the only one which does not lie completely within the feasible area. The implication of this is that although any point on the lines representing £40,000 and £70,000 is feasible, only points lying on the section BC of line AD are feasible. Any point on the section AB exceeds the land constraint, and any point on the section CD exceeds the budgetary constraint. For example, to build 480 type A houses and 19 type B would need $(480 \times \frac{1}{10}) + (19 \times \frac{1}{5})$ or 51·8 acres of land. Similarly, the cost of building 32 type A's and 200 type B's would be $[(£2000 \times 32) + (£6000 \times 200)]$ or £1,264,000.

These three features each provide a clue to how to find the optimum policy. We know that as we move away from the origin the amount of rateable value represented by each line increases. We also know that beyond a certain point there are some lines which lie outside the feasible area. What we want to find is the line which is farthest away from the origin, while keeping at least one point in the feasible area. Because the lines are parallel, we can find the optimum point by placing a ruler parallel to any of the lines we had before and moving it away from the origin until it is just touching the outer edge of the feasible area. Figure 7.6 shows the optimum policy which was found in this way. The maximum additional rateable value is obtained by building 300 type A houses and 100 type B houses. The rateable value from this combination of house types is £104,000 $[(300 \times £190) + (100 \times £470)]$. Notice that there is only one point on the line which is feasible. All points to the left or right of the optimum point violate one of the constraints.

It is possible to check that the optimum combination ($A = 300$, $B = 100$) is feasible, by substituting these values into the constraints equations.

E*

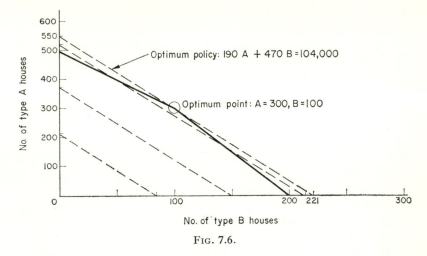

No. of type B houses

Fig. 7.6.

We know that $\frac{1}{10}A+\frac{1}{5}B$ must not exceed 50 acres, and $2000A+6000B$ must not exceed £1,200,000.

Evaluating the expression for the land constraint first, we find that:

$$\tfrac{1}{10}(300)+\tfrac{1}{5}(100) = 50$$

so that the land constraint has not been violated (nor is there any unused land).

The budgetary constraint then becomes:

$$2000(300)+6000(100) = 1,200,000$$

which means that this constraint has also been satisfied. This represents the optimum policy because the line representing rateable value cannot be moved any farther to the right without leaving the feasible area altogether.

It was implicitly assumed in this example that A and B are either zero or positive. This seems fairly obvious, because we can't actually build a negative number of new houses, so that in thinking about the problem we automatically dismiss negative numbers. However, if the problem were to be solved algebraically, it would be possible for negative numbers to emerge in the process of the solution. It is usual, therefore, to make an explicit condition that no variable should be negative, by introducing addition constraints, called non-negativity constraints. We can now re-state our simple example in standard linear programming terms:

(1) Maximise $190A + 470B$ (the objective function, rateable value)

(2) Subject to $\frac{1}{10}A + \frac{1}{5}B \leq 50$ (the problem constraints)

$$2000A + 6000B \leq 1,200,000$$

(3) And subject to $A \geq 0$, $B \geq 0$ (the non-negativity constraint)

It is possible (and just as easy) to solve problems by the graphical method where the objective function is to be minimised rather than to be maximised. If, for example, the objective was to minimise total cost, the feasible space would be constructed, and one of the lines representing a particular cost level would be drawn, and then moved *towards* the origin until it just touches a corner of the feasible area: that point is the minimum cost solution.

The graphical approach to the solution of linear programming problems can cope quite easily with two variables and a number of constraints. It can just about deal with three variables, by the use of three-dimensional diagrams. But when many variables and constraints are involved, graphical methods are not capable of providing a solution, and mathematical methods must be used. The reader who is interested in following up these methods can find a simple exposition in Battersby (1966), and a more comprehensive approach in Loomba (1964) and Vajda (1960).

When using algebraic methods the computation which is necessary to arrive at the solution can become very heavy if there are more constraints or larger numbers of variables (in our example, house types or even other buildings which contribute to rateable value). But it is perfectly straightforward, and can be easily handled using standard computer programs. The limitations of linear programming methods in planning will not generally be ones associated with the mathematical solution of the problem. They are much more likely to be related to the restrictive assumptions which a linear programming formulation entails, and to the difficulty of defining an objective function which is realistic in planning terms. It is therefore appropriate that we should spend some time considering the major problems and limitations of linear programming as a planning tool.

PROBLEMS AND LIMITATIONS

The objective function

It is obvious from the previous discussion that the first basic requirement of a linear programming formulation is the need to state a unique and well-defined objective. The overall objective of planning is clearly related to the maximisation of social and economic welfare, but this doesn't help very much, because "the construction of a meaningful social welfare function is a complex question which no social scientist would claim to have solved" (Ben-Shahar, 1969). The tendency is to look for very simple objective functions, the easiest possible solution being to minimise or maximise some single variable (such as construction cost, travel time, or accessibility). It is of course possible to extend the scope of the objective function by including a linear combination of objectives: for example, we might try to minimise something like:

$$aB + bR + cW + dS$$

where B = construction cost of new buildings,

R = construction cost of new roads,

W = journey to work,

S = journey to shop.

The Land Use Plan Design Model developed by the South-East Wisconsin Regional Planning Commission (Schlager, 1965) determines the area of land, by major land-use category, to be developed in each zone. The objective function relates to the cost of developing land for given land uses:

Minimise $C_t = C_1 X_1 + C_2 X_2 + \ldots + C_n X_n$

where the variables (X) represent residential, industrial or other land uses in given areas and the parameters (C) the costs of developing this land. It is therefore possible to specify quite complex objective functions.

To date, however, there have always been at least two important classes of variables which have been omitted from the objective function. One of these is the general class of phenomena such as amenity or aesthetics whose objective measurement is difficult, and whose effects on consumer satisfaction are even more elusive. Another has to do with social goals and social effects; many of these aspects of a problem receive implicit or explicit consideration in the political planning process but are excluded from computer solutions through oversight or convenience. However, these are limitations associated with all models, whether of the optimising type or not. More important perhaps is the fact that even the simple objectives involve a large amount of subjectivity. Parry Lewis observes:

"The choice of aim is itself subjective: but even if we have chosen to minimise the journey to work we must ask how to measure it? Do we do it in time, distance, cost, some mixture of these, or what? Do we take mean time along a route or modal time? Do we pay more attention to time spent by certain kinds of workers? Do we value time saved on a five-minute journey as much as on a twenty-minute journey? It is possible to go on listing more questions of this type. What we have to realise is that whether we ask them or not, we do in fact imply answers to all of them by our very choice of objective function. We simplify away the question, but not the answer. And as long as any one of the implied questions remains incapable of being answered objectively, so the so-called 'objective function' is objective only in the sense that it states an objective—not in the sense that it has been objectively chosen. Furthermore, even if and when all of these questions can be answered objectively, that we have chosen to consider journey to work rather than, say, rateable value, is itself probably a subjective decision" (Lewis, 1969).

The solution which is occasionally adopted to the problem of defining an adequate objective function, is to alter the solution which optimises the objective function subject to the stated constraints, to take account of certain factors which have not, or cannot be included in the linear programming formulation. This can be a dangerous procedure, and small adjustments can lead to very large departures from the "optimal" solution. Parry Lewis concludes that "until the planner can say precisely what it is that he is seeking to maximise (or minimise), the use of optimising techniques other than for purely exploratory purposes is bound to result in a simple minded plan" (Lewis, *op. cit.*).

While endorsing this warning, it does not seem to be wise to hold up the development of optimising models until we understand everything about all the possible criteria. There is a strong possibility that by working with optimising models and the plans that they produce, the planner will be able to take part in a learning process. Since a plan from an optimising model may violate some principle one knows about, but has not expressed or incorporated in the model, feedback will force one to try to express it, and it may then be possible to include it in the model.

The requirement of linearity in the objective function and constraints

We have already seen that the objective function and the constraints must be linear, i.e. the variables must be related by addition only, and with constant coefficients. In practice many of the coefficients are unknown, and where they are known, are known to be variable. Moreover, for many of the variables—especially costs of various kinds—the assumption of linearity is obviously not met in practice: if costs were linear, for example, a redevelopment scheme applied to half of an area would cost half as much as if it were applied to the whole area. This is unlikely in practice, when one considers the fixed costs and economics of scale likely to be involved in urban development. Schlager, however, suggests that the linear objective function is not a severe limitation, because "the inaccuracies introduced by a linear approximation of costs may be less than the errors of cost estimation (Schlager, 1964). However, he does agree that non-linear constraint relationships present a more serious problem, as many design standards are inherently non-linear (e.g. density standards), and when a design model is not able to satisfactorily provide for a design standard, it loses most of its usefulness.

The need for continuous variables

Another inherent disadvantage of linear programming is the need for continuous rather than discrete values for the variables specified in the model. As Schlager observes: "Land use variables and land use design choices are by nature usually discrete rather than continuous" (Schlager, 1964). The basic elements of land-use design are usually the residential area rather than the individual house plot; industrial land-use units tend to be industrial zones rather than individual factory sites. Whereas it is always possible to round off the continuous variable solution to provide a discrete solution, this rounded discrete solution may not always correspond with the continuous optimal solution.

Some of the limitations associated with linear programming can be overcome by the use of Dynamic Programming techniques (Bellman, 1962) or non-linear programming, but these are very much more complex approaches, the solution procedures for which are not yet standard, and can be very expensive in terms of computer time. However, it is capable of dealing with non-linear situations, and with discrete variables, thus removing two of the main restrictions of linear programming.

In spite of their current limitations, the prospects for optimising models seem to be promising. As mathematical and computer techniques improve, many of the restrictions of linear programming techniques can be expected to be resolved. Optimising methods could then allow the planner to become really familiar with the design problem. One could run the model many times, adopting varying design standards and different estimates of requirements. This would allow the planner to ascertain the sensitivity of the plan to variations in forecasts, and to see the effect of each set of design standards on the form and cost of the plan. Chadwick (1971) reviews some of the more advanced applications of optimising methods, and suggests how they may be used in a much more flexible manner within the planning process.

REFERENCES

BATTERSBY, A. (1966) *Mathematics in Management*. Pelican.

BELLMAN, R. (1962) The basic concepts of dynamic programming, in *Recent Developments in Information and Decision Processes*, by Machol and Gray. Macmillan.

BEN-SHAHAR, H. *et al.* (1969) Town planning and welfare maximisation. *Regional Studies*, vol. 3.

CHADWICK, G. F. (1971) *A Systems View of Planning*. Pergamon.

LEWIS, J. P. (1969) *Mis-used Techniques in Planning: Linear Programming*, Occasional Papers No. 1, Centre for Urban and Regional Research, University of Manchester.

LOOMBA, N. P. (1964) *Linear Programming: An Introductory Analysis*. McGraw-Hill.

SCHLAGER, K. J. (1964) Simulation models in urban and regional planning. *Technical Record, South-Eastern Wisconsin Regional Planning Commission*, Wankesha, Wisconsin, vol. II, no. 1.

SCHLAGER, K. J. (1965) A land use plan design model. *Journal of the American Institute of Planners*, May.

VAJDA, S. (1960) *An Introduction to Linear Programming and the Theory of Games*. Methuen, Wiley.

CHAPTER 8

Conclusions

PREVIOUS chapters have examined some of the models which have been developed and used to predict the location of urban activities. Some of the limitations and problems of these models have been mentioned already. The purpose of this final chapter is to take a general look at the adequacy of such models, and to suggest some of the ways in which urban models need to be improved. To provide a framework for the discussion, brief examination will be made of the major characteristics of urban systems. This will enable an assessment to be made of the broad requirements which a model of the urban system should meet. This is of critical importance, for the prime consideration in devising or selecting a model for use in a planning context is that the model should be capable of reproducing the phenomena or the problems in which the planner is interested. This may seem an obvious point but, as we will see later, it is one which has frequently been overlooked or disregarded in the past, often because of technical limitations on our ability to handle complex situations.

THE CHARACTERISTICS OF URBAN SYSTEMS

An urban region can be regarded as a complex socio-economic system. The essential characteristics of such a system, in so far as they affect our ability to reproduce their behaviour in a simulation model, are:

(i) They contain a large number of variables, many of which must be

130

preserved in disaggregated form if the essential interrelationships amongst them are to be preserved.

(ii) Many of the variables and sub-systems are connected by feedback relationships, and it is these interconnections which give rise to the dynamic behaviour of urban systems.

Decisions and events cannot be considered in isolation, for the sequence of individual and corporate decisions changes the environment, which itself provides the information for future decisions. It is unlikely that any attempt to reproduce (model) the behaviour of urban systems which does not incorporate the essential feedback and interaction between the system components can ever be successful in unravelling the complex chain of cause and effect in urban phenomena, because the system as a whole will behave in a way which cannot be deduced from an examination of the parts separately.

(iii) The previous paragraph suggested that urban systems exhibit dynamic behaviour because the components of the system interact. However, the dynamic nature of urban systems also derives from the fact that the feedback relationships operate over time, and the way in which they operate is likely to change with time; moreover there are invariably delays, or lags, in the ways in which the system components react to change. A basic requirement of a realistic simulation therefore must be the ability to incorporate time as a variable in the structure of the model, in order to be able to trace the performance or behaviour of the system through time.

(iv) The majority of the relationships in social and economic systems are non-linear. In a linear system, changes within the system in response to external pressures are purely additive. For example, in a linear model the cost of developing an area of 200 acres for housing must be assumed to be twice the cost of developing an area of 100 acres, and half the cost of developing an area of 400 acres, whereas in fact economies of scale are likely to give rise to a non-linear relationship. Whereas it is possible in some cases to make linear approximation to non-linear behaviour, the restrictions of linear approximations impose severe constraints on the ability of models to accurately reproduce system behaviour as much of the system behaviour that is important will be the result of non-linear phenomena. Even where linear approximation apparently enables the results of system behaviour to be determined, attempting to represent non-linear behaviour by linear approximation will frequently lead to a confusion of the cause and effect relationships, and policies based on the assumed relationships are likely to be ineffective, if not positively harmful. The ability to handle non-linearities must therefore be regarded as a basic requirement of an urban systems model.

To summarise the above discussion, the essential characteristics which an urban systems model should possess are:

   (i) the capacity to handle large numbers of variables,

  (ii) the ability to deal explicitly with sub-system interactions, and the feedback characteristics of the real-world relationships,

 (iii) the ability to incorporate time-varying relationships,

 (iv) the ability to deal with non-linear relationships.

THE CHARACTERISTICS OF EXISTING URBAN MODELS

It was suggested above that if a model is to be useful to planners, it must be capable of reproducing the phenomena or problems in which planners are interested. Because system behaviour is closely related to system structure, it follows that successful urban models will have to possess the basic structural characteristics of the urban system. This section of the chapter will not review all existing urban models in detail, but will summarise the basic features of the models previously described.

   (i) Although there are some examples of research models which contain large numbers of variables, the majority of operational models use highly aggregated variables, sacrificing the complexity and variety of the real world for computational simplicity and in some cases ease of data collection. There will, of course, always be a problem of data availability in urban modelling, and it seems inevitable that the need to reduce the number of variables included in urban models because it is not possible to obtain data will continue.

However, the reduction of the complexity of models for the sake of computational simplicity is a less desirable practice, and is largely related to the problem of obtaining analytic solutions with large numbers of variables, especially when many of these have non-linear characteristics. One of the reasons why linear and gravity models are so popular is that they effectively by-pass (rather than solve) this problem.

(ii) Many of the variables and relationships incorporated into contemporary urban models are essentially linear, or based on linear approximations. This is almost inevitable where the models are based on analytic solutions, because mathematical analysis is generally not capable of dealing with the general solutions to non-linear systems. Of the models which do not deal with linear relationships, by far the majority (those developed from the gravity principle) are based on inferred analogies rather than on an explicit theory of system behaviour.

(iii) With one or two exceptions (notably the many versions of Lowry's "Model of Metropolis") the currently available models are representations of parts of the urban system only, and it has proved extremely difficult to provide for the linking of sub-systems—if done at all, it has had to be done outside the models. The essential linkages and interactions between sub-systems (which are largely responsible for the dynamic behaviour of urban systems) cannot be represented by partial models of urban development.

(iv) Not only do existing models fail to take account of the feedback relationships between sub-systems, they have also largely been static (i.e. "equilibrium" or "one shot")—in other words they have not included time-varying relationships.

(v) The cumulative effect of the factors discussed above has meant that very few models of urban development have been able to base their *structure* on observed or hypothesised casual relationships. They deal with the symptoms or results of system behaviour rather than with the complex chain of cause and effect which gives rise to the dynamic behaviour of urban systems. It has also meant that the majority of models seem to reflect a rather simplistic view of the goals of the planning process.

In spite of these fairly fundamental limitations, the achievements of urban model-builders are not to be despised. As Chadwick (1971) says: "The strategy of sub-system modelling can be supported cybernetically if the alternative is an attempt at a 'general' model of a larger system which is of a monolithic nature (i.e. with no provision for delays within or between sub-systems). The strategy of sub-system modelling is also supportable, obviously, on practical grounds of time, cost, limited manpower resources, and data availability." Developments over the past five to ten years have in fact been enormous and have made significant contributions to our knowledge and understanding of the ways in which some aspects of the urban system behave. It is also unavoidably true that man must use the models he has available (whether they be mental models or computer models). Models of the type discussed in earlier chapters undoubtedly have limitations; but in many cases they represent the best that we have available.

A POSSIBLE CHANGE OF APPROACH

It may be, however, that a fundamental change of approach is necessary if progress in the field of urban model-building is to be made. On the basis of the analysis of the preceding paragraphs it is possible to suggest certain changes of emphasis which appear to be needed if we are to improve the quality of our urban models:

(i) First, we must try to develop models which are based explicity on cause and effect relationships, so that their structure resembles the structure of the real-world system.

(ii) This means that one of the most urgent needs in the field of urban modelling is the development of a model which relates the partial aspects of urban development together in an integrated framework. It is not sufficient to build partial models of each sub-system in turn; our objective must be to build a general systems model within which the interactions between sub-systems are explicity accounted for.

(iii) If we become concerned with cause and effect relationships, we are also likely to face an increasing need for disaggregation. Many of the relationships which determine system behaviour are relationships between disaggregated variables, and models which are based on disaggregation may therefore be expected to result in improved performance.

(iv) The other major change in direction which is needed is the change from static to dynamic methods. Real-world systems exhibit dynamic behaviour. It is not realistic to expect static models to reproduce essentially dynamic characteristics.

These suggestions are not made lightly. The difficulty of implementing any one of the proposed changes is substantial. However, the need to improve our understanding of urban systems is equally great. With better understanding of urban systems, better planning policies should be possible. In conclusion, the following quotation is presented for the careful consideration of the reader. It provides the justification for an interest in urban modelling and for this introduction to modelling technique.

"Men would never attempt to send a space ship to the moon without first testing the equipment by constructing prototype models and by computer simulation of the anticipated space trajectories. No company would put a new kind of household appliance or electronic computer into production without first making laboratory tests. Such models and laboratory tests do not guarantee against failure, but they do identify many weaknesses which can then be corrected before they cause full-scale disasters.

"Our social systems are far more complex and harder to understand than our technological systems. Why then do we not use the same approach of making models of social systems and conducting laboratory experiments on those models before we try new laws and government programs in real life? The answer is often stated that our knowledge of social systems is insufficient for constructing useful models. But what justification can there be for the apparent assumption that we do not know enough to construct models but believe we know enough to directly design new social systems by passing laws and starting new social programs? I am suggesting that we do indeed know enough to make useful models of social systems. Conversely, we do not know enough to design the most effective social systems directly, without first going through a model-building experimental phase. But I am confident, and substantial supporting evidence is beginning to accumulate, that the proper use of models of social systems can lead to far better systems, and to laws and programs that are far more effective than those created in the past" (Forrester, 1971).

REFERENCES

CHADWICK, G. F. (1971) *A Systems View of Planning*. Pergamon.
FORRESTER, J. W. (1971) *World Dynamics*. Wright-Allen Press.

APPENDIX

Calculation of Regression and Correlation Coefficients

REGRESSION COEFFICIENTS

As was explained in Chapter 4, the method of "least squares" involves finding the equation which fits a set of data in such a way that the difference between actual and predicted values is at a minimum. The criterion by which this is judged is that the sum of the squares of the deviations (of the actual from the predicted values) be a minimum.

If we consider a set of data, represented by n pairs of numbers $(x_1 y_1), (x_2 y_2) \dots (x_n y_n)$, and we fit a line to this set of data, the equation will be of the form

$$y' = a + bx$$

where y' is used to distinguish between observed values of y and the predicted values obtained from the equation. a and b are the regression coefficients which quantify the relationship between y and x.

For each given value of x $(x_i, i = 1$ to $n)$ there is a given value of y, and a calculated or predicted value, y', obtained by substituting x_i into the equation

$$y' = a + bx.$$

If the coefficients a and b are formed by the method of least squares, their values would have to be such that, after substituting all the values of x, into the equation, and calculating y'_i, the value of

$$\sum_{i=1}^{n} (y_i - y'_i)^2$$

is as small as possible.

The derivation of the formulae which provide the least-squares values of a and b is complex, and requires a great deal of algebra or a knowledge of calculus, both of which are beyond the scope of an introductory text such as this. The necessary formulae are:

$$b = \frac{n(\sum_{i=1}^{n} x_i y_i) - (\sum_{i=1}^{n} x_i)(\sum_{i=1}^{n} y_i)}{n(\sum_{i=1}^{n} x_i^2) - (\sum_{i=1}^{n} x_i)^2}$$

and

$$a = \frac{\sum_{i=1}^{n} y_i - b \sum_{i=1}^{n} x_i}{n}$$

where n is the number of pairs of observations, $\sum x_i$ and $\sum y_i$ are the totals of the known x_i's and y_i's, and $\sum x_i y_i$ is the total of the products of the pairs of values x_i and y_i.

Notice that it is first necessary to calculate b from the first equation, and then substitute the calculated value of b into the second equation to calculate a.

CORRELATION COEFFICIENT

The coefficient of correlation has been introduced as the means of testing the "goodness of fit" of a linear equation to a set of data. As the criterion for fitting the least-squares line is the sum of the deviations of predicted and actual values, an obvious measure of goodness of fit would seem to be in terms of the quantity:

$$\sum_{i=1}^{n} (y_i - y_i')^2.$$

If the difference between observed and calculated values is large, the fit is poor, and the value of the above term will be large. If the difference is small, the fit is good.

However, this simple method of testing for goodness of fit has one over-riding disadvantage. It is that the size of the term $\sum_i (y_i' - y_i')^2$ depends on the scale of measurement of the variable y. If, for example, y is measured in tens, the difference between actual and predicted values will be relatively small even if the fit is poor; if it is measured in millions, the difference may be very large even if the fit is good.

This problem can be avoided by comparing $\Sigma_i\,(y_i-y_i')^2$ with the sum of the squares of the deviations of the values of y_i from the average value of y. Again, the derivation of the formula is complex, and an understanding is not important. The equation for the correlation coefficient, r, is

$$r = \frac{n \sum_{i=1}^{n} x_i\,y_i - (\sum_{i=1}^{n} x_i)\,(\sum_{i=1}^{n} y_i)}{\sqrt{\left[n \sum_{i=1}^{n} x_i^2 - (\sum_{i=1}^{n} x_i)^2 \right]} \sqrt{\left[n \sum_{i=1}^{n} y_i^2 - (\sum_{i=1}^{n} y_i)^2 \right]}}$$

To find a coefficient of correlation it is only necessary to calculate the five totals, $\Sigma\,x_i$, $\Sigma\,y_i$, $\Sigma\,x_i^2$, $\Sigma\,y_i^2$, $\Sigma\,x_i y_i$ and substitute them into the equation above, together with n, the number of pairs of observations.

The important point to remember is that, if the fit of the line to the data is good, the value of r will be close to $+1$ or -1. If the fit is poor, the value will be close to 0.

Index